EASY GREEN CLEANING

Join the Safe, Effective, and Eco-Friendly Cleaning Revolution by Using Simple, Inexpensive, Natural, and Non-toxic Ingredients and Recipes to Keep Your Home Sparkling Clean!

Elizabeth Hemmings

Published By:

RevolutionBookSeries.com

DISCLOSURE:

I am not a chemist, a professional cleaner, environmental specialist, or licensed in any way to give advice about cleaning products and cleaning your home (I am not sure if you can even get a license to advise people on that sort of thing). I am also not qualified to give medical advice. Nothing in this book should be interpreted as providing any medical advice. The information and statements in this book have not been evaluated by the Food and Drug Administration or any other state or Federal agency. Any information contained in this book is not intended to diagnose, treat, cure, or prevent any disease. If you, or others who may be exposed to the methods set forth in this book have any medical conditions, you should consult with a doctor prior to using any of the information provided in this book. I have personally tested and used the ingredients, recipes, and methods in their book, and although I can vouch for the effectiveness and safety of them in my own personal use, I cannot do the same for you. While I expect you will experience similar results with cleaning and the recipes from this book, everyone cleans differently and has different cleaning surfaces, so I cannot make any representations, guarantees, or warranties regarding their safety or effectiveness when you use them. Everything should be used at your own discretion and you should always spot test in an inconspicuous area before using something on an entire surface. **Take any cautions or warnings I have in the book seriously, and if you have any concerns about something, do your own research!**

LEGAL DISCLAIMER:

This book is presented solely for educational and entertainment purposes. The author and publisher are not offering it as professional services or advice. Although, best efforts have been used in preparing this book, the author and publisher make no representations or warranties, express or implied, of any kind, and author and publisher assume no liabilities of any kind with respect to the accuracy or completeness of the contents in general and specifically disclaim any express or implied warranties of merchantability or fitness of use for a particular purpose. There are no representations or warranties, express or implied, about the completeness, accuracy, reliability, suitability, or safety with respect to the information, products, services, or information contained in this book. Neither the author nor the publisher shall be held liable or responsible to any person or entity with respect to any loss or damages caused, or alleged to have been caused, directly or indirectly, by or from the use of the information contained in this book. Every person is different and the advice and information contained herein may not be suitable for you or your situation. You should seek the advice of competent professionals, including medical professionals, before applying any of the information set forth in this book. By using the information set forth in this book you are expressly assuming all risk of loss, damage or injury to yourself, property, or to others. The use of the information constitutes a knowing and voluntary waiver of any claims against author or publisher arising from or related to the information set forth in this book and by such use you are waiving the right to recover actual, consequential, or punitive damages. Further readers of this book should be aware that websites and resources listed in this book may have changed between when this book was written and when it is read.

To contact the publisher and for information on bulk purchases, sales promotions, fund-raising and educational needs visit **RevolutionBookSeries.com.**

Print Book ISBN: 978-0-9994259-0-9

eBook ISBN: 978-0-9994259-1-6

Book Cover Designed By: CoverBookDesigns.com

Book Cover Images on Extended License Use:

Spray Bottle and Leaves by brookebecker/Bigstock.com

Tile Wall by weedezign/Bigstock.com

Internal Book Images:

Kiss Mark image Creative Commons CC0 for commercial use.

All other internal book images are created and owned by Revolution Book Series and follow the same copyright guidelines as listed in the **Copyright Notice**.

Visit **TheRevolutionBlog.com** for more healthy, eco-friendly living tips and receive our FREE **5 Step Guide to a Healthier Greener Life**!

Table of Contents

Why I am Writing a Book on Green Cleaning .... - 1 -

10 Reasons It's Important to Read this Book .... - 4 -

The Dangers of Toxic Chemicals in Our Homes .... - 11 -

    The Dangers We Know .... - 12 -

    The Dangers We Don't Know .... - 15 -

    Dangers of Toxic Chemicals to the Environment .... - 17 -

    Ensuring Safe Cleaning Products .... - 21 -

Chapter 1. Green Cleaning Your Home .... - 26 -

    10 Reasons People Don't Green Clean .... - 27 -

    Step by Step Easiest and Most Cost-Effective Way to Start Green Cleaning .... - 35 -

Chapter 2. Set Up Your Green Cleaning Tool Kit .... - 42 -

    Ingredients .... - 43 -

    Bonus Ingredients .... - 49 -

    Tools .... - 54 -

    Bonus Tools .... - 61 -

Chapter 3. Notes on Essential Oils .... - 68 -

    Essential Oil Cautions .... - 68 -

    Essential Oils Used in This Book .... - 70 -

Chapter 4. Recipes .... - 75 -

    Rosemary Lavender All-Purpose Cleaner .... - 75 -

    Citrus Vinegar All-Purpose Cleaner .... - 76 -

    3% Hydrogen Peroxide Cleaner .... - 77 -

    Homemade Soft Scrub .... - 78 -

    Liquid Dish Soap .... - 79 -

    Moisturizing Hand Soap .... - 80 -

    Electronic Cleaner .... - 81 -

    Stain Remover .... - 82 -

    Mold and Mildew Remover .... - 83 -

    Linen Spray/Air Freshener .... - 84 -

Fabric Refresher .... - 85 -

Baking Soda Air Fresheners .... - 86 -

Gunk Remover .... - 87 -

Furniture Polish .... - 88 -

Mattress Cleaner/Carpet Deodorizer .... - 89 -

Pest Repellant House Spray .... - 90 -

Non-Toxic, Air Cleaning Candles .... - 91 -

Chapter 5. Cleaning Different Areas Using Natural Products .... - 92 -

How to Disinfect Surfaces When Green Cleaning Your Home .... - 92 -

Bathroom .... - 94 -

    Bathtubs .... - 94 -

    Showers .... - 95 -

    Toilets .... - 96 -

Counter-top/Sink .... - 97 -

Doing Dishes .... - 98 -

    Cast Iron Skillet .... - 99 -

    Vitamix Blender .... - 100 -

    Wood Cutting Board .... - 100 -

Drains .... - 101 -

Dusting .... - 102 -

Electronics .... - 102 -

Floor Cleaning .... - 103 -

    Carpet .... - 103 -

    Hard Surface Flooring .... - 104 -

Glass/Windows/Mirrors .... - 105 -

Grout .... - 106 -

Kitchen .... - 106 -

    Garbage Disposal .... - 106 -

    Microwave .... - 106 -

    Oven .... - 106 -

    Refrigerator .... - 107 -

    Stainless Steel Appliances .... - 107 -

    Stove Top .... - 108 -

Laundry ....- 108 -

    DIY Dry Cleaning ....- 109 -

    Drying ....- 110 -

    Fabric Softener ....- 111 -

    Ironing ....- 111 -

    Laundry Boosters ....- 112 -

    Microfiber Cloths ....- 112 -

    Pre-Treating Stains ....- 113 -

    Water Temperature ....- 113 -

    Whitening and Brightening ....- 114 -

Mattress and Pillows ....- 114 -

    Mattresses ....- 114 -

    Pillows ....- 114 -

Pet Hair Removal ....- 115 -

Stain Removal ....- 115 -

Keeping Your Home Green and Clean ....- 117 -

    Keeping Your Home Smelling Fresh ....- 117 -

    Keeping Your Pets Clean ....- 119 -

    Keeping Your Children's Toys Clean ....- 119 -

    Keeping Your Produce Clean ....- 120 -

    Keeping Your Car Clean ....- 121 -

    Keeping Your Home Pest-free ....- 122 -

    Keeping Your Air and Water Clean ....- 124 -

Chapter 6. Tips and Miscellaneous Cleaning Hacks ....- 127 -

Chapter 7. Properly Disposing of Items ....- 132 -

Chapter 8. Conscious Consumerism ....- 134 -

Chapter 9. Conclusion – How Green Cleaning Impacted My Life ....- 136 -

10 Ways to Get Involved and Inspire Change ....- 140 -

End Notes ....- 148 -

WHY I AM WRITING A BOOK ON GREEN CLEANING

Green Cleaning is something I wish I learned about and started using much earlier in life. It would have saved me money and reduced my chemical exposure, setting me up for better health.

I remember the first time I experienced the dangers of using conventional cleaners. When I was a teenager, someone hired my friend and me to clean their rental property. Even though I always disliked cleaning and was never taught how to do it properly, I agreed because I wanted the extra money. For no good reason, other than not knowing better, we decided to close the bathroom door while cleaning one of the showers in a small bathroom with no windows. We then proceeded to use a very popular blue commercial cleaner containing ammonia with another very popular commercial cleaner containing bleach, at the same time, in the same area. Now if you are not familiar with what happens when you mix bleach and ammonia together (I don't blame you I wasn't either), it causes a chemical reaction and creates an extremely dangerous, toxic chloramine vapor. Our eyes started burning and we started choking and gagging and ran outside as quickly as we could, gasping for breath.

Given the severity of the situation, we came out relatively unharmed as it could have resulted in a trip to the emergency room. Looking back now, I realize that experience should have made me question what I was using to clean my home and why it is so easy to purchase and use products capable of creating such a toxic and harmful reaction. I didn't question it, though. I continued to use the conventional cleaning products because they were easy to buy, and I assumed, because of that, they were also safe to use.

Many years later I came across a book showing over 100 uses of hydrogen peroxide, which was a huge eye-opener for me. Not just because hydrogen peroxide could be used for so many things, but because the book really broke down the dangers of conventional cleaning products and why they are completely unnecessary for use in our everyday lives.

After that, I was hooked. I started reading and researching everything I could on non-toxic green cleaning (to an obsessive extent) and started experimenting with ingredients and recipes to see what worked best. Let's just say I fell in love with green cleaning and feel I have gained some expertise in the area, so I decided to take the next logical step by writing my own book about it.

Now you're probably asking, "Why write another book on green cleaning when so many already exist?"

I found when reading many books on the green cleaning, that most of them over-complicated the approach. Some of the more popular books advertise over 100 different recipes to naturally clean your home, which in my experience, is very unnecessary and makes it a lot more complicated than it needs to be. Other books only focused on one ingredient like using a lemon in 50 different ways. Some books just contained bad practices, including using vinegar on stone surfaces like granite, which is never a good idea. I wrote this book to address those problems and create an easier and more in-depth guide.

My primary intention with writing this book is to reach a new audience of soon-to-be green cleaners. For those of you already interested in green cleaning, I trust that you will benefit from the information and recipes here. It will solidify your understanding that green cleaning is the best way to go and allow you to benefit from the lessons I've learned and the expertise I've gained. But, I hope this book also reaches people who are not familiar with green cleaning and have absolutely no idea that it is something they want to do until they read this. It's important to me that this book not only tells you how to apply green cleaning methods and recipes but also *why*. I hope this book becomes the "start here" book you gift or recommend to your friends who are interested in green cleaning (or haven't found their interest in it yet).

A lot of research went into exposing the proven dangers of some of the most commonly used commercial cleaning ingredients and bringing light to the unknown dangers. I make strong statements in this book as green cleaning and caring for our health and the planet is something I am passionate about. Please know when reading this book that it is not meant to scare, alienate, or offend anyone. I believe it's important to understand why you are making a change.

We need to change the way we treat the planet, treat ourselves, and treat each other! Spreading the message of green cleaning is one small and doable step to achieve that goal.

I know from personal experience that transitioning to green cleaning methods is one of the easiest steps you can take in making positive, conscious changes in your life. Once the shift is made, this can catapult into more conscious changes that not only positively impact you and people around you, but also has the potential to impact the entire world. And this, is why I need your help spreading the message to convert the world to green cleaning! There is more at the end of the book on how to help do just that.

For now, let's dive into why you should read this book and how it will help you on your journey (that you may or may not have known you were on) to a clean and green home.

Let the journey begin...

10 Reasons It's Important to Read this Book

Green cleaning is a way to clean your home without all the chemicals that are either known or presumed to be toxic to you or the environment. It is about using time-tested, safe ingredients and reusable materials.

When mentioning chemicals or commercial cleaners in this book, I'm specifically referencing the ones that are known or presumed to be toxic. It's important to make the distinction that not all chemicals or commercial cleaners are toxic. It is also important to note that just because something is natural does not automatically make it safe. This book will help educate you on how to make the safest decisions for what to use when cleaning your home.

Listed below are the top ten reasons reading this book on green cleaning is important and how it can benefit you.

Reason #1: It's Simple

My goal with this book is to keep everything as simple as possible. You will not find complicated methods or recipes here, as I personally don't use them. If you see a **K.I.S.S.** mark anywhere in the book, that stands for **Keep It Super Simple,** and there will be an even simpler recipe of the full version with fewer ingredients and ingredients that are easily accessible and **only take a couple of pours and a shake to make.** I also stick to the easiest and most efficient practices when I detail how to green clean your home.

Reason #2: It Saves Time

This book summarizes what I learned over the past few years as I researched and practiced in the world of green, eco-friendly cleaning. It took lots of trial and error, as well as countless hours of research and reading various articles, websites, and many books on the subject. I compiled the research, and what I found to work best in terms of the ingredients, tools, and information, in this book. It includes my personal recipes and the cleaning techniques I found to be the most efficient and effective, along with my favorite tips and tricks. All the recipes included in this book can be made in a few minutes or less and should save you some trips to the store.

Some of these recipes and green cleaning practices are original to this book; some can be found through multiple sources online. By compiling this information, I hope to save you time in your own journey so you can get started down the path of green cleaning right away in the easiest way possible.

REASON #3: IT'S EFFECTIVE

The recipes and green cleaning practices in this book work! Since starting green cleaning, I have not encountered anything that I could not clean just as well (or better) using my own DIY (do it yourself) products along with the simple ingredients and methods listed in this book. My sheets and clothes get just as clean without the skin irritation I experienced with regular detergents. My windows and mirrors are just as streak-free without the chemical smell of the more traditional cleaners that used to make me gag. My toilets are so sparkling clean and disinfected you could eat off them (don't worry I haven't). I also enjoy cleaning much more now that I use safer products, which means my home stays cleaner.

REASON #4: IT'S HEALTHIER

There are many reasons to go green with your cleaning. The most important being that it is a lot better for your health and your family's health than conventional cleaning. The following chapter on **Dangers of Toxic Chemicals in Our Homes** gives the in-depth reasons for why this is so. I would also argue that we are only at the beginning of discovering the negative impact chemicals have on us and our loved ones. Why use cleaning products that have links to cancer, respiratory problems, and reproductive problems in your home when it is not necessary to do so? There are even concerns that these toxic cleaning products may be linked to certain cases of autism, ADHD, and birth defects.

Do you really want to play Russian roulette with your health and your family's health on whether these products are going to cause harm?

It is VERY IMPORTANT to switch to green cleaners if you have infants or small children running around. They have a greater exposure to chemicals than a fully grown adult due to their small size and having more direct contact with the surfaces you clean. When they are young they tend to climb on everything and put lots of things in their mouths. Children are also far more vulnerable to chemical exposure because their organs and immune systems are not fully developed yet, making their little bodies a petri dish for toxic chemicals.

REASON #5: IT'S ENVIRONMENTALLY FRIENDLY

"A nation that destroys its soils destroys itself..." – Franklin D. Roosevelt

"The environment is where we all meet; where all have a mutual interest; it is the one thing all of us share." - Lady Bird Johnson

"We do not inherit the earth from our ancestors, we borrow it from our children." – Native American Proverb

We all must share this planet and we shouldn't take that responsibility lightly. The chapter on **Dangers of Toxic Chemicals to the Environment** will provide more information on some of the chemicals proven to have a negative impact on our health and planet. I think it is important to note that we have only reached the tip of the iceberg (which is melting) when it comes to fully realizing the impact these chemicals used in conventional cleaners have on our ecosystem. These chemicals are very new in relation to the billions of years our planet has existed. Although we are already starting to see their negative impact, imagine 10, 20, or 100 years from now and the impact they will have if we don't decrease the environmental exposure to these products now. The more people get these toxic chemicals out of their homes, the greater the reduction of chemical build up in our soils and water supply, dampening the negative impact for future generations. This is one way you can play a role in improving the planet for all.

Another important way green cleaning helps the environment is it will dramatically reduce typical household waste. You will reuse packaging and cleaning tools you would have thrown away previously and more supplies can be bought in bulk with recyclable packaging. In addition to reducing waste, it will lessen the use of resources and chemicals that are byproducts of the manufacturing process. Replacing paper towels with reusable cleaning cloths is just one excellent way of doing that.

References mentioned in the following text box may be found at endnotes 1 and 2.[1,2]

> Paper towels are not recyclable. It takes as many as 51,000 trees per day to replace the number of paper towels that are discarded daily. To make one ton of paper towels approximately 20,000 gallons of water are polluted.
>
> It is estimated that 13 billion pounds of paper towels are used in America each year. That is the equivalent amount 45 pounds of paper towels per person, per year. That is a lot of paper towels and a huge amount of waste! If every American reduced the number of paper towels they use by just one paper towel per day, it would have the potential to save the landfill from 571,230,000 pounds of paper waste each year saving millions in dumping fees.

REASON #6: IT SAVES MONEY

You will save money by switching to green cleaning and using the methods in this book! You can make these recipes for a fraction of the cost of buying the same product from the stores. Additionally, the ingredients you buy can serve multiple purposes. No more buying a separate granite cleaner, toilet bowl cleaner, carpet cleaner, fabric softener, laundry detergent, glass cleaner, disinfectant, electronics cleaner, floor cleaner, dish soap, hand soap, air-freshener, and the list could go on! When you purchase the cost-effective, multi-purpose ingredients listed in this book, you will be able to do all those things and more. You will also be reusing most of your cleaning tools. Although the tools may cost more upfront, they are sure to save you lots of money in the long run.

REASON #7: IT'S SAFER

The most common causes of poisonings of children under the age of six are from personal care products and cleaning supplies. Many of these products come in colorful packaging and sometimes smell fruity or sweet. These exposures are almost always unintentional. When it comes to more serious poisonings, meaning poisonings that result in serious injury or fatalities, household cleaning substances rank number three under analgesics/pain killers and toxic fumes/gases/vapors according to a national statistics report published by poison.org. In addition, according to the Pet Poison Helpline, household cleaners rank in the top ten pet poisons, ranking number two for cat injuries and fatalities.

All cleaning products, natural or otherwise, should be safely stored away from children and pets. Using natural cleaning products with food-grade ingredients, like the ones in this book, greatly reduces the chance of accidental poisoning. I also took the liberty to list any additional warnings for any ingredients requiring special precautions with children and pets like essential oils. Please read the essential oil cautions in the book for more information on safe use especially if using around pets, young children, or while pregnant Natural or not, to keep your family safe, you need to have a full understanding of what you use in your home to clean with.

Although it might not be fatal in small amounts, why take the risk of having your children and/or pets playing on and eating off surfaces cleaned with traditional household cleaners? Why keep unsafe, poisonous products in your home when you don't need to?

> Your pets walk on your floors, lie on your surfaces, drink out of your toilets, lick, and chew things around your house no matter how much you tell them not to, and then lick themselves. They are more frequently exposed to these cleaning products than you are. If you don't start green cleaning for yourself, do it for them! Dogs get into everything and conventional cleaners are very toxic to them. Cats can be especially sensitive because they have an acute sense of smell, absorb cleaning products easier through their skin, and have a more difficult time breaking down harmful substances that they ingest in their liver.

REASON #8: IT'S SELF-SUFFICIENT

Acquiring more DIY (do it yourself) skills and reusable materials is a smart investment you can make in your independence. Due to unstable financial markets, turbulent government, environmental concerns, and burnout of consumption, it is a wise idea for people to have interest in self-sufficient and sustainable living. Having the ability to clean your home using raw ingredients with multiple uses and reusable materials is a good first step to a more self-sufficient and sustainable home should disaster strike.

REASON #9: IT'S EMPOWERING

Education empowers people to make positive changes in their lives. This book is not only designed to give you the 'why' but also the 'how.' I do not believe in making people aware of problems without giving them solutions.

I feel it is very important to educate people as much as possible on the harm of the chemicals around them while giving them alternatives for safer options. Although it is impossible to completely escape the exposure of toxic chemicals in your environment, reducing them as much as possible will have a very positive impact. It is about progress over perfection and having the right information to protect you and your family.

REASON #10: IT'S INSPIRING

By taking action and spreading the message of the green cleaning practices in this book, we have a real shot at affecting change.

It is not something we need government interference or corporate interests to agree with to be able to accomplish. It is not a class issue the way some other issues are when it comes to public health and safety. Rich or poor, we can all green clean as it is easy and accessible to virtually everyone. I explain some of the most cost-effective methods to do so with widely available ingredients. We have complete control and power over how we choose to clean our homes and the products we use. If enough people make the change and spread the message, we can really affect change in a major industry. To learn more about how you can inspire change, read the chapter at the end of the book **10 Ways to Get Involved and Inspire Change.** As mentioned previously, I believe green cleaning is the first and easiest step in making positive changes in your own life and in the world.

"You cannot get through a single day without having an impact on the world around you. What you do makes a difference, and you have to decide what kind of difference you want to make." —Jane Goodall

*For those of you that are not yet convinced of the dangers of toxic ingredients in conventional cleaning products and want to see more research and cited data, the next couple of sections on the **Dangers of Toxic Chemicals in Our Homes** and **Dangers of Toxic Chemicals to the Environment** written by a contributor are for you.*

THE DANGERS OF TOXIC CHEMICALS IN OUR HOMES

The U.S. Environmental Protection Agency (EPA) defines a toxic chemical as any substance which may be harmful to the environment or hazardous to your health if inhaled, ingested or absorbed through the skin.

It would be irresponsible not to acknowledge the significant contributions chemistry and certain chemicals have made to society. However, it is also to our detriment to not question the effects, both short and long-term, of new, "helpful" compounds brought into the consumer marketplace. These new, artificial creations are just that; new. In an article published by *Wired* magazine, it is stated, "Humans have found or made 50 million different chemicals here on Earth, the vast majority over the last few decades."[3] While it took 33 years to create the first ten million compounds, it now takes less than nine months to create ten million more.[4] And while not all new things are inherently bad, as a society we must pause to consider the full ramifications of these products, which in many cases, have been found to do significant harm or sometimes even worse, have not been tested at all.

The National Research Council cites, "less than 20% of chemicals in every-day use products have been tested for acute effects and less than 10% have been tested for chronic, reproductive or mutagenic effects."[5] This finding should be startling, but I don't expect you to take my word for it. The purpose of this chapter is to explore some of the less-publicized studies on the effects our household chemicals cause; and some that have not been studied at all. I hope to provoke thought into this relatively unexplored area and to encourage you, the consumer, to know your options when bringing chemicals into your life and your home.

THE DANGERS WE KNOW

As children, we are taught from an early age to avoid many household cleaning products, as ingesting these products can lead to a trip to the emergency room or worse. According to the Center for Disease Control (CDC), more than 300 children are admitted to the emergency room each day because of accidental poisoning.[6]

Listed below are a few of the most pervasive household cleaners and the compounds found in these cleaners that have known human health risks associated with their use on a consumer basis.

CHLORINE BLEACH

Chlorine bleach is one of the oldest "modern" chemical cleaners, with its discovery dating back to the 18th century. While people have been utilizing chlorine bleach around the world for hundreds of years, its negative effects should not be taken lightly. According to the New York Department of Health, "When chlorine enters the body as a result of breathing, swallowing, or skin contact, it reacts with water to produce acids. The acids are corrosive and damage cells in the body on contact."[7] Anyone who has ever worked with chlorine knows its smell to be pungent and might not be surprised to read that the acids created are corrosive or damaging, but the dangers of chlorine should not be ignored. Chlorine has been found to, "alter and destroy unsaturated essential fatty acids (EFAs), the building blocks of human brains and central nervous systems."[8] In addition, the presence of chlorine has been discovered to create a higher rate of miscarriages in women, artery damage, and increased rates of melanoma and cancer.[9]

Due to its toxic properties, chlorine was used as a chemical weapon in World War I. It worked so well they used it again in World War II.

VOLATILE ORGANIC COMPOUNDS (VOCs)

According to the National Institute of Health (NIH), volatile organic compounds, known as VOCs, "are organic compounds that easily become vapors or gases. Many volatile organic compounds are commonly used in air fresheners, detergents, rug and upholstery cleaners, aerosol sprays, furniture polish, degreasers, oven cleaners, and dry-cleaning fluids."[10]

The NIH states VOCs are pollutants that deteriorate air quality. In large amounts VOCs create holes in the ozone layer of the atmosphere. People are exposed to VOCs both outdoors and indoors. Benzene and formaldehyde, two common VOCs in cleaning products, are known carcinogens. "Long-term exposure to volatile organic compounds can cause damage to the liver, kidneys, and central nervous system. Short-term exposure to volatile organic compounds can cause eye and respiratory tract irritation, headaches, dizziness, visual disorders, fatigue, loss of coordination, allergic skin reactions, nausea, and memory impairment."[11]

PHTHALATES

Unlike chlorine, you might not recognize the name "phthalates" right off the bat, but rest assured you encounter these compounds every day. According to the NIH, phthalates are defined as, "a group of chemicals used to soften and increase the flexibility of plastic and vinyl..."[12] They are found in so many products it is hard to list them all, but they are frequently found in anything that is fragranced. This means that not only are they found in personal care products like shampoos and perfumes, but also in your household cleaning products like air fresheners, fabric softeners, and laundry detergents.

Why are phthalates a problem? Phthalates are known endocrine disruptors in both males and females. Studies show phthalate exposure in males leads to low sperm count and testicular cancer, among other health problems.[13] The same study concluded a statistically significant portion of pregnant women exposed to phthalates had shorter gestational periods (premature births) than those who were not exposed.[14]

By the NIH's description, phthalates have made their way into a veritable assortment of consumer goods. They are found in pretty much anything fragranced such as detergents, fabric softeners and air fresheners. However, if you check your product labels to see if the product contains phthalates, be aware that, in many cases, law does not require the presence of those compounds to be disclosed on the product label.

In 2005, the New York Times ran an article explaining the loophole: "[When a company brings a product to market] their formulas are considered proprietary secrets, so the manufacturer may simply use the generic term 'fragrance'"[15] instead of disclosing what ingredients the item is formulated with. Hiding the presence of phthalates under "fragrance" may make you think, "I'm in the clear because I buy unscented." But even with unscented products, phthalates are routinely incorporated to mask the natural occurring scents.[16]

AMMONIA

Ammonia is a frequently occurring ingredient in household cleaners because of its streak-free shine properties. The New York Department of Health describes it as having a "pungent, suffocating odor."[17] A descriptor like that alone may be enough for some to rethink its presence in the home, but rest assured there is more evidence to back it up. Ammonia is so effective at its job because it evaporates quickly. This means that human exposure to ammonia is also through inhalation of ammonia vapors, rather than just contact to the skin.

The inhalation of ammonia vapors can lead to, "bronchiolar and alveolar edema (the buildup of fluid in the lungs), and airway destruction resulting in respiratory distress or failure. Inhalation… can cause coughing, and nose and throat irritation."[18] The Department of Health importantly notes ammonia's strong smell provides early warning of its presence, but after time can also "olfactory fatigue or adaptation," meaning a person's ability to recognize the presence of the smell decreases over time, thus making them less aware of the damage it's causing.

Ammonia alone is enough to cause some legitimate issues, but ammonia in combination with any chlorine-based products (another common cleaning agent) creates an entirely different beast. When ammonia and chlorine are mixed, due to accidental contamination or otherwise, a toxic chloramine gas is formed. One study found that "exposure to chloramine gas represents a substantial risk when household cleaners containing bleach and ammonia are mixed." In this instance, "upper-airway irritation can compromise the airway and require an emergency tracheostomy."[19]

THE DANGERS WE DON'T KNOW

The list of known dangerous chemical additives can go on and on, but there is also something to be said for the fact that in comparison to the total body of chemicals out there, very little or nothing is known about the short and long-term effects of a shocking percentage of the chemicals available in today's market. During the research for this chapter, I scoured dozens of scholarly articles and sources for evidence to support these claims related to concerns with toxic chemicals in household and cleaning products. Excerpted below are a few of the instances in which the studies found that inadequate information existed to determine conclusive results, either for or against the presence of a chemical:

*"Expanded research is needed into the environmental causation of autism. Children today are surrounded by thousands of synthetic chemicals. Two hundred of them are neurotoxic in adult humans, and 1000 more in laboratory models. **Yet fewer than 20% of high-volume chemicals have been tested for neurodevelopmental toxicity**."*[20]

*"**Additional studies are critically needed** to help elucidate possible explanations for differences across studies, and most importantly, to address whether phthalate exposure alters semen quality, sperm function, and male, fertility."*[21]

*"Fragranced consumer products are pervasive in society. **Relatively little is known about the composition of these products, due to lack of prior study, the***

complexity of formulations, and limitations and protections on ingredient disclosure in the U.S."[22]

*Referencing cleaning products: "These products can contain chemicals that are not disclosed to the public through product labels or material safety data sheets... Results point to **a need for improved understanding of product constituents and mechanisms between exposures and effects."[23]***

*"Efforts to identify the contribution of specific products to home environments or personal exposure are hindered by the **limited and inconsistent disclosure of chemical ingredients in consumer products."[24]***

The results of these studies or lack thereof should spark considerable concern into the safety of commonly accepted chemical compounds and cleaning ingredients. As shown above, in many cases the lack of disclosure of these chemicals directly hinders the ability for professionals to accurately study the effects, both short and long-term, on human health. Furthermore, in many instances studies have started too recently to provide valuable results. Yet, we have been using these products, without being clear on their health impacts.

After reading pages and pages of reports and studies regarding chemicals in household products and cleaners, I was left with a lot of questions, and seemingly few answers. I had to wonder:

1.) Why do so many people, and at one time myself included, feel so comfortable bringing these products into their homes without knowing how thoroughly the impact of the ingredients has been studied or for what period?
2.) Should we use certain chemicals when inadequate information exists to determine conclusive results regarding their safety?
3.) Are there potential risks that outweigh the benefits?

It seems distinctly possible the potential unknown risks do, in fact, outweigh the surface-level benefits many common products are perceived to have. I personally feel it is not worth the risk to bring under-researched products into the home and this motivated to dive into green cleaning.

In today's climate, consumers face an uphill battle in becoming informed on the nature of the chemical ingredients they bring into their home. It is my wholehearted belief that by beginning to understand the ramifications of some of these ingredients and the current limitations in scope and longevity of studies, consumers will begin to be more aware of their chemical surrounds and demand more answers.

It is my hope this book will give you some of the information to help you take control of what you choose to bring into your home, and that it sparks your interest in being more informed as to what is in the products you purchase. As a result, I hope informed consumers create a need for the cleaning industry to be more transparent with the overall impact of their products.

DANGERS OF TOXIC CHEMICALS TO THE ENVIRONMENT

The multitude of health issues caused by chemicals found in common household cleaners is striking. However, your personal health is not the only safety concern to keep in mind. The environmental repercussions for using these chemicals can be vastly detrimental to both local ecosystems and the global atmosphere. Just as we only have one body so we must take care of it, we only have one earth to call home, and we must take great care of it as well. This section will delve into some of the negative effects some of these compounds found in common household cleaners have on the environment.

PHTHALATES

Phthalates, found in many cleaning products as mentioned in the previous section, are nothing to take lightly. Phthalates also significantly affect the environment. Phthalates can enter the exterior environment through waste-water (household runoff) and leeching from landfills. Once phthalates enter waterways, their detrimental effects begin. Like the endocrine-disrupting concerns phthalates may create in humans, the evidence of the impact on the environmental level is strong. Since the 1980's, concern has raised regarding the effects of chemicals found in water runoff and their effects on wildlife. In one example, across the United States and abroad, phthalate-laden runoff has been found to be the cause of feminization of male fish; meaning that male fish are growing female eggs.

A study done by scientists at the US Fish and Wildlife Service and the US Geological Survey found "An astonishing 60 to 100 percent of all the male smallmouth bass they examined had female egg cells growing in their testes."[25] Another concerning takeaway scientists found with this study is that these affected fish were all found in protected waters, therefore the contamination of the water is more widespread than previously believed. "When fish are getting intersex, it's probably a good indication that something is wrong in the environment," says Vicki Blazer, a researcher at the U.S. Geological Survey's National Fish Health Research Laboratory in West Virginia.[26]

VOLATILE ORGANIC COMPOUNDS (VOCS)

VOCs are commonly found in household cleaning products such as air fresheners, paint thinners, degreasers, and dry cleaners among many others. These compounds are considered "volatile" as they are readily vaporized at relatively low temperatures. VOCs play a role in environmental concern due to their ability to aid in the creation of ground level ozone.

Ozone occurs in the stratosphere and in the troposphere. The stratosphere extends about 30 miles from the earth's surface, whereas the troposphere accounts for the air in the first five miles or so near the surface of the earth (ground level). The ozone layer in the stratosphere protects us from ultraviolet radiation. This is where the depleting ozone occurs, creating a hole that has concerned the scientific community. However, we also need to be concerned when ozone is created in the troposphere (ground level ozone) as according to the US Environmental Protection Agency (EPA), "Breathing ozone can trigger a variety of health problems, particularly for children, the elderly, and people of all ages who have lung diseases such as asthma."[27]

When VOCs interact with nitrogen oxides (NOx) and sunlight at the tropospheric level they undergo a chemical reaction to create ozone.[28] The EPA also states "Ground-level or 'bad' ozone also damages vegetation and ecosystems. It leads to reduced agricultural crop and commercial forest yields, reduced growth and survivability of tree seedlings, and increased susceptibility to diseases, pests, and other stresses such as harsh weather. In the United States alone, ground-level ozone is responsible for an estimated $500 million in reduced crop production each year. Ground-level ozone also damages the foliage of trees and other plants, affecting the landscape of cities, national parks and forests, and recreation areas."[29]

By limiting the use of VOCs found in cleaning products and other items, we can help slow the creation of detrimental tropospheric ozone.

PHOSPHATES AND AMMONIA

Phosphates (a form of phosphorous) and ammonia (a form of nitrogen) are chemical additives found in detergents, and many products are advertised respectively, coming with a multitude of environmentally hazardous effects; namely being major aids in eutrophication. Eutrophication may sound like a long and complicated word, but if you have spent much time by the water, you may be familiar with the term "red tide" indicating there is a harmful algal bloom. Nitrogen and phosphates are essential in aiding plant growth; they are the two most potent ingredients in fertilizers. However, nitrogen and phosphorus' effects on land plants are not equal to its effects on aquatic plants and algae. Nitrogen's effects on aiding the growth of aquatic plants are significantly stronger than land-based plants. Therefore, even trace amounts of nitrogen and phosphorus in bodies of water can easily cause the flare up of algal blooms.

Algal blooms can be harmful in several ways. Some types of algae produce toxins as they grow, effectively killing the wildlife in and around the surrounding waters. Other, non-toxic, algae can still cause harm when it blooms in excess levels as well. When the non-toxic algae are given enough nutrients to grow rapidly (as caused by nitrogen eutrophication), the algae frequently grow in high density near the surface of the water so it can best photosynthesize. While the algae are blooms near the surface, it effectively cuts off the amount of sunlight that can reach the deeper depths of the body of water. The deeper aquatic plants are then not able to absorb enough light to photosynthesize. Therefore, the deeper aquatic plants die, which is a two-pronged hazard to the surrounding aquatic life. Some aquatic life will suffer due to a diminished source of food if they relied on aquatic plants as part of their diet. The other, and often more serious, element of this ecological event is that when the aquatic plants begin to die, the decomposition process removes the dissolved oxygen from the water. Dissolved oxygen is naturally occurring and is what fish "breathe" through their gills. As the plants rot and dissolved oxygen is eaten away by the decomposition process, the surrounding fish have no more oxygen left to breathe and suffocate, resulting in massive death events of the aquatic life. The National Oceanic and Atmospheric Association states, "Every U.S. coastal and Great Lakes state experiences HABs [harmful algal blooms]. These blooms are a national concern because they affect not only the health of people and marine ecosystems, but also the 'health' of our economy — especially coastal communities dependent on the income of jobs generated through fishing and tourism."[30]

Due to the massively negative environmental impact and consumer push back, phosphates have, been banned from laundry detergents in all states in the United States and have been banned in a little over a dozen states currently for use in dishwasher detergents. Huge progress has been made in this area but there is still a significant way to go to get them completely out of people's homes. Ammonia, on the other hand, has not been banned in any states and remains common in household cleaning products.

CHLORINE

Chlorine is commonly found in household cleaning agents, most typically in bleach. When chlorine becomes present in waste-water, such as the water that runs off from household drains, it easily combines with other compounds to form dioxins and chlorinated organic compounds. According to the EPA dioxins are, "highly toxic and can cause cancer, reproductive and developmental problems, damage to the immune system, and can interfere with hormones."[31] Dioxins are highly susceptible to bioaccumulation, meaning they are easily stored in the fatty tissues of aquatic life, and as smaller fish are consumed by larger animals in the food chain, huge levels of dioxins can be found in the larger fish. This brings bad news for both fish and humans alike as humans frequently unknowingly consume large amounts of dioxins when eating larger fish such as those that are harvested for sushi and other seafood products. When chlorine combines with other substances, it can create any one of a variety of chlorinated organic compounds such as chlorinated fluorocarbon or chlorinated hydrocarbon.

According to a study done on the toxicity of chlorinated organic compounds, "many chlorinated compounds are toxic to man and animals. Their genotoxicity (mutagenicity and carcinogenicity) plays a role in risk assessment; more and more chlorinated organic compounds are being shown to be carcinogenic."[32] Additionally, like other VOCs, chlorine is a compound that, when it becomes exposed to ultraviolet light (sunlight), will react with ozone atoms and destroy them, effectively worsening the strength of the very necessary ozone layer of our stratosphere.

The chemicals listed above are only a few of many that negatively impacted our environment. While some are released only in small amounts at a time, they frequently linger in the earth for sustained periods and build potency as more chemicals are released. By becoming aware some of the damage these chemicals are known to cause, hopefully, you can now make more informed decisions about choosing whether you feel comfortable bringing them into your home.

ENSURING SAFE CLEANING PRODUCTS

The last two sections showed you a few primary chemicals in conventional cleaning products with harmful impacts on your health and the environment. Those are not the only ones you should be concerned about.

Here are several other common chemicals in cleaning products you should be aware of because of their environmental and health concerns. Even though these ingredients may not be listed on the label, they are very common in most conventional cleaners.

FORMALDEHYDE – Commonly found in many conventional cleaners and disinfectants. Has very high evidence of being carcinogenic (having the ability to cause cancer) in humans and some evidence that shows it can be harmful to aquatic life. [33]

2-BUTOXYETHANOL – Commonly found in glass cleaners, stain removers, carpet cleaners, oven cleaners, and rust removers. Strong evidence that it causes red blood cell damage and hemolytic anemia in animal studies. Animal studies also show it can cause liver damage.[34]

SODIUM HYDROXIDE – Commonly found in oven, drain, toilet, and stove top cleaners. Causes severe skin burns and eye damage and can cause respiratory problems.[35]

TRICLOSAN – Triclosan has been banned from hand soap but can still be found in many everyday products including cleaning supplies. It has high evidence of being very toxic to aquatic life. It has also shown the risk of promoting bacterial resistance.[36]

Even "green cleaners" you purchase have chemicals in them that can cause negative effects. I feel they are still safer options for cleaning your home, but making your own cleaning products, as I will lay out in this book, is one of the best ways you can ensure you are cleaning your home with safe and effective products. When purchasing any cleaning product even "greener cleaners" you should ask yourself:

What level of toxicity are you willing to tolerate?

You may be thinking you are not that susceptible to these toxins because you are just cleaning with these products and not swallowing them. Swallowing cleaning products is not the only way they can get into your body. They can also be absorbed through your skin and respiratory system.

References mentioned in the preceding text box may be found at endnote 37.[37]

> The EWG did a study utilizing different laboratories in the United States to examine the umbilical cord blood of ten different babies. They found more than 200 industrial chemicals in each newborn. Many of the chemicals found have been shown to cause cancer, be toxic to the brain and nervous system, and cause birth defects or abnormal development in animal tests. This demonstrates the multitude of ways chemicals can enter your body and how serious the implications are.

You may be asking, "If these chemicals are so bad why is the government not protecting us and allowing these harmful chemicals into our products in the first place?"

There is a lot of complexity to that question, and a deep dive into the discussion would warrant a separate book, but for the purposes of breaking it down into simple terms, I do my best to explain below.

For further reference visit **TheRevolutionBlog.com/cleaning-references.**

A lot of new chemicals were brought into the marketplace in the United States after the World Wars to keep the industries, previously used to create chemical warfare, afloat. With all these new chemicals becoming household standards, they had to find a way to regulate them. A law was enacted in 1976 called the Toxic Substances Control Act (TSCA). It was put in place to regulate chemicals that were not previously covered under other statutes. One of the big problems with this law when it was first enacted, was that it allowed approximately 62,000 chemicals already on the market at the time to continue to be used without safety testing. Any chemicals after that time were allowed to stay on the market unless the Environmental

Protection Agency (EPA) could establish "unreasonable risk." The chemicals and products on the market were considered innocent until proven guilty. The other problem here was the law only give the EPA 90 days to prove unreasonable risk with the way it was written. The EPA rarely had all the toxicity data they needed during that time to effectively uncover and prove negative impacts or toxicity of these products. If they could not prove a product was harmful in that time period the product was found appropriate for the market and consumers even though it was not proven to be safe for people and the environment. Other countries governing groups like the European Union have much stricter chemical laws and have banned well over 1,000 chemicals vs. the EPA which has banned less than a dozen chemicals to date via the TSCA.

Some progress was made to the TSCA in 2016 by giving extra time to prove unreasonable risk, requiring more testing, and allowing the chemicals that were "grandfathered" in to be investigated further.

This progress is great, but let's be honest, it could take years or decades to see results and chemicals pulled off the market, even with the progress we are making today. But, as consumers, we have the power to make decisions now by what we purchase. We can take a stand by not purchasing the products containing toxic chemicals. We can vote for what we want on the shelves by what we purchase.

An even bigger problem faced by consumers is the lack of disclosure on what is contained in the cleaning products. Since cleaning products are not regulated by the Food and Drug Administration (FDA), due to not being food, drinks, or drugs ingested by humans, manufacturers are not required to list all ingredients of these products and can keep many private under the guise of being "Trade Secrets." Manufacturers are only required to list ingredients of "known" concern. This leaves a big caveat, when in the past, they have not required testing to confirm which chemicals have a "known" concern. In addition, unlike the food industry, there are few guidelines when it comes to labeling personal care or cleaning products. This means that terms like "non-toxic," "natural," "environmentally friendly," and "biodegradable" hold virtually no meaning, as their definitions are not regulated by any governing group.

How can consumers make educated decisions for themselves when they are not always being fully told what is in their products? **There needs to be more transparency here as people have the right to know what they are bringing into their homes.**

The bottom line: If you want to use products that you know are safe, it is best to make them yourself or purchase from a company you trust as many "green" products on the market today label it as such as a marketing ploy, but the product still contains harmful chemicals because they can.

What is Greenwashing?

Greenwashing, according to an online dictionary, is the "disinformation disseminated by an organization so as to present an environmentally responsible public image." Now there are many reputable companies out there that are doing what they can to have a positive impact, but there are also many companies that use greenwashing to project an environmentally responsible image when that is not really the case. Make sure you know what a company's true values and processes are if you intend to purchase from them for the sake of being green.

CHAPTER 1. GREEN CLEANING YOUR HOME

Now that this book explained the importance and benefits of green cleaning, the upcoming chapter sections will give you the how including: what to purchase, how to make your own green cleaning products, and how to use them.

But first, let's review and banish any of the excuses or reasons people give for not green cleaning. In the chapter titled **10 Reasons People Don't Green Clean,** I go into some of the reasons people give for not green cleaning and how to address them. If you are not yet convinced to green clean, please read this chapter.

I also have a chapter on **Step by Step Easiest and Most Cost-Effective Way to Start Green Cleaning** to walk people through the best way to do it if they are not ready to dive right in and not sure where to begin.

I hope this book becomes a resource that you continue to come back to. The tools and ingredients are listed with pictures and descriptions for easy reference. I highly recommend you refer to the tools and ingredients chart if you are going to purchase or use them, as I list cautions and other important points.

The cleaning processes are all searchable through the table of contents, making it is easy to find the recipe or information you need when you need it.

The **Tips and Miscellaneous Cleaning Hacks** chapter includes additional things I learned throughout my own green cleaning journey that did not appropriately fit anywhere else in the book. I felt these tips were worthwhile to include, so, if you are looking for how to clean something and don't see it listed in the table of contents, check out this chapter.

Throughout the book, I refer to links where you can find recommended resources for the ingredients and products mentioned. You can find all products and ingredients mentioned in the book at **TheRevolutionBlog.com/cleaning-resources.**

Additionally, you will find additional helpful links and references like recommended books, documentaries, and helpful websites to help you find other pieces of information that will assist your own green cleaning journey, such as where to recycle certain items in your area, and how to find a green dry cleaner at **TheRevolutionBlog.com/cleaning-references.**

Anytime you see a kiss mark and the abbreviation K.I.S.S under a recipe, it stands for Keep It Super Simple and will provide a simpler version of the recipe above that takes the least amount and most simple ingredients to make.

Even if you do not read this book in its entirety, I highly recommend you read the concluding chapters on **Conscious Consumerism**, **Conclusion - How Green Cleaning Has Impacted My Life**, and **10 Ways to Get Involved and Inspire Change**. These chapters contain very good information to help inspire and motivate you on your journey.

10 REASONS PEOPLE DON'T GREEN CLEAN

When I was writing the first draft of this book and distributing it for feedback, I was shocked to find that I hadn't converted everyone to immediately start green cleaning. Having worked with green cleaning products for years and knowing how easy and effective they are to use, I assumed that after reading about green cleaning each reader would be itching to get all those toxic cleaning products out of their homes. That was not necessarily the case. I was still getting push back from many people and I started asking them why. This chapter on **10 Reasons People Don't Green Clean** reviews some of the reasons or concerns people gave me for not changing to green cleaning. This chapter also attempts to get ahead of the reasons for not green cleaning, so, hopefully, none of them hold you back from a cleaner, safer life.

REASON #1: CONDITIONED TO USE THE COMMON COMMERCIAL PRODUCTS

Although no one specifically states this as their reason for not green cleaning, it needs to be addressed as an underlying cause as to why so many people are addicted to their toxic products and chemical cleaners. These products have been used to clean the average family home for a long time. They have been marketed to us through commercials, ads, and strategic product placement, conditioning us as a society to think using these products is necessary for a clean home. In addition, most of us were raised with these chemical cleaning products used in our homes, so, we tend to use the same cleaning products throughout our lives.

I once heard a joke about cutting off the sides of the turkey before cooking being passed down from generation to generation. When the great-grandmother comes over for Thanksgiving dinner, she asks why the sides of the turkey are cut off. They explain it is because that is the way the great grandmother always did it when they were growing up. She responds with, "That is because her oven was too small to fit the whole turkey."

My point being, people often do things without necessarily having a good reason or knowing why, but just because they have been conditioned to do it that way from the people that raised them. My primary goal with this book, is to arm young adults with the knowledge of green cleaning, so that when they first move out on their own, they never take these toxic products into their homes, promoting the ways of green cleaning to be passed down from generation to generation.

> Habits and routines are another way people feel stuck in their ways. Keep in mind that by green cleaning you are not changing the way you clean, but are changing what you clean with. It is like brushing your teeth. Changing your toothpaste does not change the habit you created of brushing your teeth, but the right toothpaste may allow you to enjoy it more and see more benefits.

REASON #2: YOU MAY BELIEVE GREEN CLEANING IS TIME CONSUMING

The number one push back I got is people feel it will be time-consuming to green clean and make their own cleaning supplies. Trust me, it is not. I only include easy and simple recipes in this book that take a few minutes or less to make. Most recipes also feature a K.I.S.S. sign recipe. The K.I.S.S. mark stands for Keep It Super Simple and features a recipe with very few, easy to find ingredients only taking a couple pours and a shake to make. As I keep the ingredients for my most common recipes on hand, I find it saves me time quickly mix up my Rosemary Lavender All-Purpose Cleaner for instance as opposed to running to the store to find a suitable cleaner.

Also, time is all about prioritization. With all the hours many of us spend browsing social media, watching TV, and surfing the internet, if green cleaning is a priority, we can afford to spend 10-20 minutes a month (or less) making our own cleaning supplies that are better and safer for us and our family. If you are inspired to make your own cleaning products but still feel like time is an issue, keep in mind you can make the products (& clean) while watching your favorite TV shows or while listening to a podcast, audio book, or something you enjoy.

Some people also feel it will be a hassle to buy all the ingredients and more work to use the DIY (do it yourself) products. But, I will argue it is not any more of a hassle to buy the ingredients than to purchase all the different cleaners people commonly use. It is also no more of a hassle to use them as they are just as quick and effective as conventional cleaning products. If, for some reason, you still are not ready to give making your own cleaning products a shot, at least switch to greener, safer versions of the cleaning products you do buy.

Can't I just clean my house with regular soap and water?

The short answer is that you can clean your house with just soap and water. A spray bottle filled with water and a couple of squirts of Castile soap or an ecological plant based dish soap is a very simple and environmentally friendly way to clean and is very hassle-free. I don't personally use that method because it does not have the same disinfecting properties as many of the recipes I lay out in this book. Also, using soap of any kind can leave a film, but I still think it is a great way to green clean if you experience effective results from using it. Just make sure whatever you use to wipe down the surfaces is clean or you are just spreading more bacteria and germs around your house during the cleaning process.

REASON #3: YOU BELIEVE CONVENTIONAL CLEANERS ARE NECESSARY AND MORE EFFECTIVE

I could talk until I'm blue in the face about the effectiveness of green cleaning products and the recipes in this book, but the only way to know for sure is to try them out for yourself. The ingredients and products mentioned in this book are effective at disinfecting surfaces, absorbing odors, and even adding a fresh scent. Under the ingredients section I provide more information on what makes these ingredients and recipes effective.

Even after everything that is addressed about the dangers of certain chemicals in conventional cleaners, people seem to have the most difficult time believing that they could replace the following conventional cleaning products and still clean effectively:

AMMONIA BASED GLASS CLEANER - It seems like people believe ammonia is needed for a streak-free shine on glass and mirrors. This is not the case. There are several recipes in this book that can provide a streak-free shine. You can use pretty much anything that is vinegar or alcohol-based to achieve streak-free results. I will say one of the big secrets to getting a streak free-shine is by using a microfiber or other lint-free reusable cloth. From my experience, using an ammonia-based cleaner with paper towels never got my glass or mirrors as streak-free as using the recipes in this book with microfiber cloths has.

CHLORINE BLEACH - This can be a tough one for people to give up. People feel they need bleach to whiten whites and to disinfect surfaces. I provide studies and examples later in the book on how surfaces can be disinfected just as thoroughly using the recipes in this book as with chlorine bleach. For now, I will just discuss the whitening topic. Chlorine whitens whites by eating away at your fabrics (while also eating away at your skin and respiratory system). Based on personal experience as someone who is obsessed with only buying and sleeping on white sheets, and who used to be an avid bleach user, I can vouch that my sheets stay white and last a lot longer using the **3% Hydrogen Peroxide Cleaner** than they did when I used chlorine bleach. To keep white items white, I always add some **3% Hydrogen Peroxide Cleaner** to the wash and, sometimes, I pre-soak with it as well. I pre-treat any stains using the **Stain Remover** recipe. I have been so happy with the results of this process that I would never go back to using chlorine bleach again.

Some people associate the intense smell of chlorine bleach and ammonia-based glass cleaner with the smell of clean, thinking that it shows their effectiveness. But, that is not the smell of clean. These smells are meant to serve as a warning that you are being exposed to poisonous gasses and to be cautious. If you are looking for a true clean smell, wait until you try cleaning with essential oils – they have many antibacterial, antimicrobial, and antifungal properties, plus they smell amazing!

REASON #4: YOU HAVE FAVORITE CONVENTIONAL CLEANING PRODUCTS

I was talking to a friend about writing a book on green cleaning. She mentioned that when her first child was born she switched all her products to green cleaners, but no longer uses them and went back to conventional cleaning products. When I asked why, she said it was because as effective as they were, it was really difficult for her to give up her favorite laundry detergent. She said since she switched back to the conventional detergent, she felt there was no point to keep cleaning with the other green supplies when she was already bringing toxins back into her home.

People seem to take an all or nothing approach with a lot of things in life. Instead, I encourage people to look at it from more of an 80/20 or 90/10 approach. If you have a favorite conventional cleaning product you are not ready to give up, do not let that hold you back from making the switch in other areas. You will still reap many benefits from making the switch to other products and you may, one day, decide you are ready to commit to change 100% of your products. You also don't need to remove all your conventional cleaning supplies from your home right away. Put the conventional supplies in a box and know they are there if you need them until you are 100% sure you are ready to make the transition.

REASON #5: YOU BELIEVE IT'S EXPENSIVE TO SWITCH

You may have the belief that switching to green cleaning is expensive because, when purchasing products in stores, the greener, eco-friendly cleaners tend to cost more than conventional cleaners. However, green cleaning is actually very cost effective, in fact, you can save money by easily making your own cleaning products for a lot less than purchasing them (even cheaper than the conventional cleaners). Nonetheless, you may still worry about the upfront costs to get these new ingredients and supplies. But, you probably already have a lot of the ingredients and tools at home or can pick them up easily and inexpensively the next time you go to the store instead of purchasing your regular cleaners. You can effectively green clean your home using just the basic K.I.S.S. recipes in this book, which require very few tools and ingredients. You can always invest in other ingredients and supplies at a later point, using the money you saved from not purchasing expensive one-use cleaning products.

Once you invest in the upfront supplies, you will be able to make all the cleaning products you need for a year at fraction of the cost of what the average family spends on conventional cleaning products in a year.

REASON #6: YOU WORRY IT'S HARD TO FIND INGREDIENTS OR TOOLS

I do my best to make this easy for you by listing all ingredients and tools that are easily found, including where to buy them at TheRevolutionBlog.com/cleaning-resources. All the basic ingredients and everything used in the K.I.S.S. recipes are probably already in your home or can be found at the same local store you purchase your regular cleaning supplies from. Buying the most frequently used ingredients in bulk is a great way to ensure you always have them around. If you want to dive right in, this book also includes a comprehensive list in the **Set Up Your Green Cleaning Tool Kit** chapter of the supplies you may want for the recipes and practices used in this book.

REASON # 7: YOU DON'T LIKE THE SMELL OF VINEGAR

A handful or people cite the smell of vinegar as one of the main reasons they are turned off from green cleaning (others are fine with it). I would like to point out vinegar is actually a good odor neutralizer that helps to get rid of other wanted smells, and the smell of vinegar itself dissipates quickly. I personally associate the smell now with the smell of clean. I would also like to add, many conventional cleaners do not smell great either (and are not healthy to breathe in).

However, I can understand people not wanting to use vinegar for cleaning and you definitely do not have to use vinegar to green clean your home. You can use any of the vinegar-free cleaners to effectively clean your home with excellent results. While there may be some recipes for specific applications that call for straight vinegar for smaller jobs, you can choose to omit these recipes or you may find them tolerable since they do not require vinegar being sprayed all over your house. My point is that vinegar is not necessary for whole-house green cleaning.

If you want to use vinegar but still have an issue with the smell, you may find that masking the smell of vinegar with essential oils or infusing some lemon or orange peel into the vinegar may be enough for you to comfortably use it for green cleaning.

REASON # 8: YOU FIND IT INTIMIDATING OR OVERWHELMING

My hope is this book makes green cleaning simple and more approachable. I certainly cover a lot of information with everything I have learned in my green cleaning journey, but my intent is to make this a reference book you can come back to repeatedly as you progress down your own green cleaning path. I understand how information overload can make it seem like an overwhelming process, so I do my best to break things down into simple steps and recipes, which is the best place to start when getting started with green cleaning before diving into some of the other suggestions. If you are looking for the simplest and easiest recipes to get you started, begin with the K.I.S.S. recipes you will find in this book.

REASON #9: YOU DON'T THINK IT MAKES A SIGNIFICANT IMPACT

It does make an impact! I sincerely hope after reading this book in its entirety you realize just how important green cleaning is for your health and the health of the planet. It is not worth it for you, your family, your pets, or anyone else to be exposed to such toxic products. Even if you don't have pets or kids, the risk to you is not worth it; especially when it is such an easy change to make for your own health and well-being.

Small differences go a long way in keeping you and the environment safe. Reducing your waste and toxic burden on the planet is important for everyone to do. These products work to make your home cleaner and healthier, and to cut down on your household waste significantly. Toxic cleaning products need to be taken very seriously. If enough people make the changes in the book and spread the message of green cleaning, it will force the companies making these toxic products to quit treating our bodies and the planet like chemical dumping grounds; something the current laws and regulations have not been able to accomplish. Please do your part to progress the green cleaning movement forward, as we need the majority to be able to make a difference. To put it bluntly, people's lives and the future of our planet depend on it! Even the small steps make a difference. Perhaps you do not directly control the cleaning products used at your work, at your children's school, or other places you commonly frequent, but you can control what is used within your home & green cleaning reduces your (and the planet's) overall exposure to toxic chemicals.

REASON #10: YOU DON'T KNOW WHERE TO START

The next chapter provides a simple step by step process of the easiest and most cost-effective way to get started. Please dive in!

"A journey of a thousand miles begins with a single step." – Lao Tzu

STEP BY STEP EASIEST AND MOST COST-EFFECTIVE WAY TO START GREEN CLEANING

"Success will never be a big step in the future: Success is a small step taken just now." – Jonatan Martensson

I'm the type of person who goes full-force into something I'm passionate about. Green cleaning was no exception. I quickly started buying all the ingredients and tools to start completely green cleaning my home in one fell swoop. I realized, while some people may decide to do the same, for many others making these changes is going to be a more gradual process. Whether you plan to dive in head first or take a more gradual approach, created this step-by-step guide to the easiest and most cost-effective way to start green cleaning.

STEP 1: TAKE INVENTORY OF WHAT YOU ALREADY HAVE ON HAND

As mentioned, a lot of the ingredients and tools listed in the following chapters may be ones you already have on hand. Take inventory of what you already have at home and make note of what you need to purchase. The base ingredients needed for the K.I.S.S. recipes, which are discussed more in the following chapter, are white vinegar, distilled water, vodka or rubbing alcohol, 3% hydrogen peroxide (make sure it is fewer than 6 months old), baking soda, and either Castile soap or a simple mild dish soap to use in its place. Also, check to see if you have large spray bottles on hand that you can use to mix the recipes. Plastic bottles are fine. Glass bottles are only needed if you are using for essential oils. You may already have enough things to make some of the K.I.S.S. recipes or you may need to wait until you go to the store.

K.I.S.S. Shopping List

- ☐ **Baking Soda**
- ☐ **Distilled White Vinegar**
- ☐ **3% Hydrogen Peroxide**
- ☐ **Vodka or Rubbing Alcohol**
- ☐ **Castile Soap or Ecological Dish Soap**
- ☐ **Distilled Water**
- ☐ **Spray Bottles**
- ☐ **Reusable Cleaning Cloths**

STEP 2: STOCK UP ON BASE INGREDIENTS

Next time you visit your local store, stock up on some of the base ingredients and consider buying them in larger sizes than you normally would. Buy the largest bottle of vinegar and the largest package of baking soda you can find. Warehouse stores can be a great place to get these items in bulk inexpensively once you are ready to purchase in bulk. If you don't already have it on hand, purchase a large bottle of 3% hydrogen peroxide and rubbing alcohol or cheap vodka at your local liquor store. If you can find Castile soap, that is great. If not, a mild dish soap can be used in the place of Castile soap in all the recipes except hand soap and pet shampoo. If you do not already have spray bottles on hand, purchase those as well. It is not a good idea to reuse plastic spray bottles that previously held toxic cleaning products because the toxins could have leached onto the plastic and could contaminate the green cleaner.

STEP 3: MAKE THE K.I.S.S. (KEEP IT SUPER SIMPLE) RECIPES

Start with making the recipes listed in the book with a K.I.S.S. mark with the ingredients you now have at home. Replace some of your most commonly used products with the newly made simple green cleaners. If you have ample ingredients at the ready, you may choose to make some of the full recipes, but if you don't, I recommend you start with the basics to get a feel for green cleaning. A good recipe to start with is one of the all-purpose cleaners that can be used on a majority of surfaces in your home.

STEP 4: BOX UP YOUR OLD CLEANING PRODUCTS

Box up the conventional cleaning products you replaced with your newly created, greener recipes. Store them in a safe location where you can still access them if necessary until you are ready to get rid of them for good and properly dispose of them. That way, you will know where they are if you really need them and have them as a safety net as you adapt to green cleaning. You may not have been able to replace all conventional cleaners at this point, but just continue to add them to the box as you start replacing them with greener options.

STEP 5: USE REUSABLE CLEANING CLOTHS

Although it is a small investment up front, purchasing microfiber cloths will save you a lot of money in the long run by drastically reducing your paper towel use. Microfiber also takes your green cleaning game to the next level. Microfiber clothes provide a streak-free shine and trap the dirt within the fibers so nothing is left behind. They naturally combat germs, and although the green cleaning products in this book can be used with them, you do not want to use them with any conventional cleaners. You can, however, use them with just water and still reap the grime-cutting and germ-fighting benefits. An alternative to investing in microfiber cloths is to use old rags or cut up t-shirts as reusable cloths. They won't have the exact same cleaning power but will still do a great job and a much better job at cleaning surfaces than conventional paper towels.

> The thrift store can be a great place to get old rags or t-shirts to cut up if you do not already have them on hand.

STEP 6: START PURCHASING OTHER INGREDIENTS AND MAKING FULL RECIPES

Start adding some more of the specialty ingredients listed in the chapters below to your green cleaning arsenal. You can then begin experimenting by making some of the full versions of the included recipes. You may find some new favorite cleaning products in making these recipes; I did. If you start using essential oils at this point, you need to invest in some glass spray bottles and may decide to add some other specialty green cleaning tools in at this point as well. You may also want to start purchasing more ingredients in bulk to save even more money.

> An alternative to purchasing glass spray bottles is to use the green glass bottles that sparkling mineral water often comes in. They fit a spray nozzle and still provide some protection to light exposure. Glass vinegar bottles work well too but do not provide the same light protection that is preferred when working with essential oils.

STEP 7: START REPLACING MORE CONVENTIONAL CLEANERS

By now, you may be fully invested and entirely green with your cleaning, or you may find yourself with some conventional cleaning products you are having a hard time giving up. Now that you are more familiar with green cleaning and know its effectiveness, it is a good time to see if you can find replacements for some of the cleaners you have had a hard time letting go of – either via the recipes and methods in the book or by purchasing greener options. If, after trial and error, you still feel you need to hang on to those last few products, go ahead and do so until you feel motivated to make the switch.

> For a long time, I was obsessed with the smell of a very popular fabric softener. It was not until I read somewhere that washing items with conventional fabric softener was a danger to cats if they lie on those items washed with it and then lick themselves that I decided to stop using it. I loved my cat way too much to take the risk. That fabric softener never made it back into my cleaning routine again.

STEP 8: GREEN YOUR CLEANING SERVICES

Now that your personal cleaning routine is nice and green, it is time to make the switch to other services you use for cleaning purposes. See if you can find an eco-friendly dry cleaner that is PERC (perchloroethylene) free. Switch to a chemical free carpet cleaner that just uses steam or natural cleaners if you do not clean your carpets yourself. If you use a cleaning service, get them a copy of this book, and insist that they use the products and ingredients in this book. You should have the green products ready for them to clean your home or ask them to prepare them.

STEP 9: GET RID OF CONVENTIONAL CLEANERS

Once you feel comfortable and have fully made the switch, go ahead and get rid of the box of chemical conventional cleaners, but make sure you dispose of them properly. I wrote a whole chapter called **Properly Disposing of Items** toward the end of the book, so be sure to reference that when removing the box from your home.

STEP 10: START LIVING A GREENER LIFE

Now that you are officially green cleaning, you may decide you want to green other areas of your life as well. There are so many other areas where you can make conscious changes, including your food supply, personal care products, water quality, gardening, and the products you bring into your home. Maybe you will feel inspired to recycle more, start composting, or support other important environmental causes. The most important thing is to take it one step at a time and not overwhelm yourself. I have never felt or looked better than I have after starting to live consciously and making these changes in my own life. I also feel proud that I am doing my part toward a healthier world.

You do not need to make massive changes overnight. This is not about being perfect. You can choose to start taking small steps or big steps. The important thing is to just start taking steps. I think one of the main problems many good causes face is that they tend to alienate the people who do not go full force into the change or ignore some of the smaller changes people do make for the cause. My goal here is to not alienate anyone. It is about bringing people together for a common goal of a healthier, safer, kinder world. You should be proud of yourself for any step you personally take in that direction.

"Sometimes the smallest step in the right direction ends up being the biggest step in your life. Tip Toe if you must, but take the step." – Naeem Callaway

Another way to dip your toe into the green cleaning pool is just to start with one or two of the full recipes or K.I.S.S. versions of the green cleaning recipes in this book. For starting out, I highly recommend the **Rosemary Lavender Cleaner** as it is very effective and safe for pretty much all surfaces. I also recommend the **Homemade Soft Scrub** as a good starting point for seeing the effectiveness of green cleaning in areas that have more grime. Once you have made those recipes, consider putting a spray nozzle on a purchased bottle of 3% hydrogen peroxide to add extra disinfecting when cleaning things like toilets and bathtubs.

Throw in some microfiber cloths for their cleaning power and streak-free shine ability and you are well on your way to creating a clean and green home.

Changes can multiply if you start with just one product!

One person who received a pre-distribution copy of the book took a while to get started but, finally, made the Rosemary Lavender All-Purpose Cleaner. She had been mainly using paper towels and water on her granite counter-tops to avoid chemicals and dishrags. The microfiber cloths and all-purpose cleaner left her counters shiny and sanitized. She found it was inexpensive and easy to make the cleaner and would give it, along with a few microfiber cloths, to some friends who also ended up loving the product. A professional cleaner was also given the solution and liked it so much that she wanted to make the products and advertise herself as a "Green Cleaner." These examples of green cleaning being passed on are perfect examples of what this book is all about.

CHAPTER 2. SET UP YOUR GREEN CLEANING TOOL KIT

When storing these ingredients and the cleaning supplies you create, be sure to select a cool, dark place away from pets and children, especially where precautions are indicated for children and pets.

You should always test an area before cleaning it when introducing any new cleaning product and make sure the ingredients used are safe for that type of surface. If using any of the cleaning recipes mentioned on carpet, fabric, or other porous surfaces, it is always a good idea to do a small spot test first in an inconspicuous area.

To find recommendations on all ingredients and tools listed in the following sections visit **TheRevolutionBlog.com/cleaning-resources.**

Green Cleaning Superstars: These are the primary ingredients and most used multi-taskers in the green cleaning arsenal.

INGREDIENTS

BAKING SODA (SODIUM BICARBONATE)

Baking soda is inexpensive, safe, easy to find, and works as an effective but gentle abrasive and natural deodorizer, making it a green cleaning superstar. Baking soda is one of the ingredients you will want to buy in bulk due to its many uses in green cleaning.

CASTILE SOAP

Castile soap is a simple, vegetable-based soap that is more ecological than a lot of the other detergent-based liquid soaps. Castile soap has many uses in both cleaning and personal care. It is a safe, mild cleaner that can be used in place of other liquid soaps and detergents. When buying Castile soap, I highly recommend you buy the unscented variety and use your own essential oils to add fragrance, if you desire. Castile soap is another ingredient that can be more expensive when not purchased in bulk, but to start out you may want to purchase a small bottle. You can use an ecological plant-based dish soap in its place in most recipes. Castile soap is a concentrated product, so a little goes a long way.

DISTILLED WATER

It is preferable to use distilled water instead of tap or filtered water in the recipes you will be storing because they will last longer. Tap water has bacteria and other contaminants you don't want to clean with, which are removed through the distilling process. In addition to removing harmful substances, distilling water also removes salts and minerals so that it and does not leave any residue or streaks on the surfaces. To remove bacteria you can boil the water then let it cool before using. If you still prefer to use plain tap or filtered water feel free just use within a month and switch to distilled if you notice streaks.

ESSENTIAL OILS

The essential oils I use for the recipes in this book are lemon, orange, rosemary, lavender, peppermint, and tea tree due to their powerful cleaning and disinfecting properties. Please feel free to substitute any essential oils you prefer to use. For more information about essential oils, please read the **Notes on Essential Oils** section, including the cautions to be aware of when using the oils. Although effective and fun to work with, do not let not having essential oils keep you from using the recipes in the book. The products you make will still be effective without them.

Hydrogen Peroxide is a disinfecting and cleaning powerhouse with many uses. This is what I use to replace chlorine bleach in my cleaning routine, and I highly recommend you do the same. Hydrogen Peroxide breaks down into water and oxygen when it hits our water systems. It does not have the negative environmental impact that chlorine does. I personally recommend food grade hydrogen peroxide over the regular drug store type because it does not have the fillers the drug store version does and can be used in applications that directly touch food. However, you can use the drug store brand in all applications listed in this book that do not directly touch food. Purchasing 3% Food Grade Hydrogen Peroxide can be expensive, so that is why the recipe in this book calls for 35% that is then diluted to 3%. Hydrogen Peroxide should be stored in a cool dark place, but I never recommend storing in the refrigerator. It must be kept in an opaque bottle like the one it comes in. Once the solution is purchased at 3% or diluted, it should be used within six months. You can use Hydrogen Peroxide on virtually any surface, but I always recommend you spot test on any porous surface. You cannot use hydrogen peroxide on silver and copper because it will cause it to oxidize.

***35% Hydrogen Peroxide is very caustic, meaning it can burn and should be handled with

extreme care using protective glasses and gloves. Whenever talking about using hydrogen peroxide to clean anything in this book I am always talking about using a 3% solution, which does not have the same caustic effect. Store 35% away from pets and kids.

SOAP NUTS (SOAP BERRY)

Soap Nuts are the shells of berries that contain saponin, making them a natural detergent. In Ayurvedic medicine, soap nuts (also known as Aritha) have been used to treat eczema and psoriasis due to their natural antifungal and antibacterial properties. They are non-toxic, sustainable, and affordable. They can be reused several times and composted when done. Soap nuts are another superstar with multiple cleaning and personal care uses, but my favorite being for laundry because they are so mild, gentle for clothes, good for fabrics, and ideal for babies and people with sensitive skin. They are not actual nuts, so people with nut allergies should have no problem using them. They can also be used in all types of washing machines and are ideal for high-efficiency machines because they do not produce a lot of bubbles or foam. You want to make sure you purchase soap nuts with the seeds removed.

Vinegar

Purchase regular distilled white vinegar in the largest jug you can find. Vinegar has many uses in green cleaning, so it's a good idea to stock up. Vinegar both disinfects and deodorizes, which is why it is such a great all-purpose cleaner. It is also great at descaling mineral buildup. The smell of vinegar dissipates quickly and removes the smells that existed before it, making it such a great deodorizer. You should not use vinegar on natural stone counter-tops like granite, quartz or marble, stone tile, or waxed floors, due to the acidic nature of this product. Do your research before using on different types of wood and finishes as well. It is safe for use on sealed grout if it is rinsed after.

Vodka/Rubbing Alcohol

Go to the liquor store and buy the biggest, cheapest bottle of vodka made from grain you can find. Vodka is a powerful disinfectant and deodorizer with multiple cleaning purposes. It is safe for natural stone and most surfaces, unlike vinegar. I prefer vodka as an ingredient instead of rubbing alcohol because rubbing alcohol (isopropyl alcohol) is not consumable and is more irritating to the skin and respiratory system than vodka. If you feel uncomfortable having vodka in your house, feel free to substitute with rubbing alcohol instead. The exception to this is I do not recommend rubbing alcohol for any sprays used for fabrics due to its more potent smell and potential respiratory irritation. The reason alcohol has been used in the past on cuts and scrapes is because of its amazing ability to kill germs, bacteria, and viruses, making it a great ingredient to clean with. It also makes a great preservative.

Bonus Ingredients

Not completely necessary but a bonus to have in your green cleaning stash.

Beeswax

Beeswax is only needed if you choose to make the candle recipe. To keep it easy, I highly recommend you purchase beeswax pastilles instead of a block of beeswax so it's easier to measure and you don't have to spend your time grating it. Not only is natural beeswax non-toxic, but some people state the negative ions produced by beeswax helps clean the air. If you have asthma or allergies, it is worth researching more about the benefits of beeswax candles as they can be very helpful for those conditions.

Honeybees that pollinate much of the food we eat are disappearing at an alarming rate. Purchasing local and ethically sourced beeswax and honey is one small thing you can do to help protect the honeybee population.

CORNSTARCH

Cornstarch is great at absorbing grease and oil and is a great additive for a natural glass cleaner for an extra streak-free shine. It is also a natural way to make a starch solution for ironing. If allergic to corn you could swap with another starch alternative like arrowroot.

DRIED HERBS AND FRUIT PEELS

These ingredients are not necessary but can be a good addition to the air fresheners and sachets. Examples of dried herbs to use are lavender, rosemary, peppermint, and bay leaves. Cedar chips can also be nice to use in areas where you want to repel moths. Lemon and orange fruit peels can also be used in your green cleaning routine.

GRAPEFRUIT SEED EXTRACT

Grapefruit seed extract is used as an optional ingredient in some of the recipes. It is a powerful natural, antimicrobial, antiviral, and antifungal agent. It is used in the recipes to add more disinfecting power and help preserve the product. Some of the main compounds in grapefruit seeds (known as limonoids and maringenin) act as antimicrobials and antioxidants, killing dangerous microbes while providing a preserving effect. It's another ingredient that can be used for cleaning, personal care, and health remedies.

LEMONS

I don't think it's practical to use lemons for everyday cleaning, and I prefer to use lemon essential oil instead, but they are a great natural bleaching agent, disinfectant, and smell great. Limes are another good ingredient to disinfect with, and they smell fantastic as well.

OILS

Oils like olive, coconut, and almond can be used in your cleaning routine to help polish things like wood and stainless steel, remove gunk and stickers, and add a moisturizing component to your hand soap.

SALT

Remove the table salt from your pantry where it has no business being (swap with unrefined sea salt), and move it into your cleaning cabinet. Regular table salt can be used for multiple purposes but is especially beneficial used as a scrub when you need something more abrasive than baking soda.

SODIUM PERCARBONATE

Sodium percarbonate is what many people refer to as oxygen bleach. Sodium percarbonate is soda ash and dry stabilized hydrogen peroxide. It is the ingredient in popular oxygen bleaches without the fillers or high price tag. It needs hot water to be activated and should be used with caution. It always needs to be diluted and should never be consumed. This is another ingredient you will want to store with special care away from pets and children.

Vegetable Glycerin

Vegetable glycerin is good at distributing essential oils in products and has a moisturizing effect, which is why it is used in the hand soap as an optional ingredient. It can also help remove stains and add slickness to surfaces to make them easier to clean like shelves in a refrigerator. Glycerin is a completely optional ingredient and has more use in personal care than cleaning.

TOOLS

The tools listed are an important part of the green cleaning routine and making the included recipes. They help reduce waste, and items like microfiber cloths and scrub brushes work so much better than their conventional counterparts.

For more information on where to purchase the green cleaning tools mentioned visit: **TheRevolutionBlog.com/cleaning-resources**

BROOM/DUSTPAN

A broom and dustpan are necessary basic cleaning tools.

DISH BRUSHES

Dish brushes are more sanitary and less wasteful than sponges. They can be thrown in the dishwasher regularly to be kept clean. Just make sure you get one with nylon bristles that is safe for nonstick or ceramic pots and pans. These brushes can be used for more than just dishes, and I recommend having several to use for different things.

DRYER BALLS

Dryer balls are a great reusable and toxin-free replacement to dryer sheets. They improve softness, shorten drying time, and help reduce static. I recommend using wool ones but plastic ones are also available.

FLAT-HEAD MOP

A flat-head mop is better and more sanitary than a traditional mop head since it covers more space and the removable cloth cover can be thrown in the washing machine. The mop can be used with a spray cleaner as opposed to a bucket, which is easier and more sanitary. Keep plenty mop covers on hand so you don't have to wash them too often.

GLOVES

Gloves are a must-have for any cleaning routine. Even though these cleaning ingredients are non-toxic, they can still be drying to your hands, and let's face it, some of the stuff you need to clean is gross and you probably don't want to touch it with your bare hands anyway.

LABELS OR LABEL MAKER

You will want to label your products. You can either buy basic labels you hand write or type on, chalkboard labels for a cute flair, or invest in a label maker.

MICROFIBER CLOTHS

Microfiber cloths can be used to replace most of your paper towel use. They work much better than paper towels when it comes to cleaning as the fine fibers do a superb job at cleaning and germ removal! I recommend you use multiple colors for different areas of your house. More about this in the tips and hacks section. Keep enough on hand so you only need to wash them once or twice a month, and wash them after each use, unless you are doing a simple wipe down, then you can use several times before washing. As much as I love the cleaning power and streak-free shine you get with microfiber cloths, feel free to use any reusable rag or cloth of your choice. ****Please see note under Laundry section in regards to washing microfiber in a way that won't cause "microfiber pollution".**

MUSLIN/MESH CLOTH BAGS

Muslin or mesh cloth bags are reusable for various purposes and are used in this book to put soap nuts in and create fragrance sachets.

PAPER TOWELS

Although reusable microfiber cloths can significantly reduce your paper towel use, you will still need to use them for things like wiping down toilets, cleaning things like litter boxes, or soaking up greasy messes. Use paper towels sparingly, and consider buying recycled paper towels to help save trees.

SCOURING SCRUB CLEANING PADS

Scouring pads are still a great addition to green cleaning. These are not for everyday cleaning, but they can be great to use when more abrasion is needed to get the job done than baking soda or microfiber cloths provide. I like to cut each pad into thirds and discard after a few uses. They do have greener alternatives to the typical green scouring pads including ones made out of agave fibers or walnut shells. There are reusable alternatives available as well that are top rack dishwasher safe.

SOAP DISPENSERS

Glass soap dispensers are preferred to plastic and used for hand soap and dish soap. You can choose a regular or foam pump top.

SPRAY BOTTLES AND MISTERS

To create your all-natural cleaners, use cobalt blue or amber glass bottles for anything containing essential oils. Plastic can be used for anything not containing essential oils. Make sure the plastic spray bottles you use are #1 PET or #2 HDPE, which do not contain BPA. Most of the regular spray bottles you can buy for cleaning are made from those plastics so they should not be hard to find. For some of the products, you may just need to use the spray nozzle and may need to cut down to size.

TOILET BOWL BRUSH

The toilet bowl brush is another necessary basic cleaning tool. Make sure it has its own holder for storage so it doesn't come into contact with other cleaning tools or surfaces.

VACUUM

It is highly recommended that you use a vacuum with good suction and a HEPA filter for cleaner air.

Bonus Tools

These tools are not necessary but great to add to your green cleaning routine.

Candle Making Supplies

To avoid burning petroleum-based candles in your home, you can make your own natural beeswax candles. If you make candles, you will need 100% cotton wicks and a metal pitcher in addition to the beeswax. With beeswax, you want to use a thicker wick so #4 is the recommended size or larger if you use a larger container. I highly recommend having a metal pitcher that you only use for candle making as anything you melt wax in can be tough to clean.

Charcoal Air Fresheners

Charcoal air fresheners are great at absorbing odors. They use activated charcoal inside a breathable pouch or container. Activated charcoal absorbs odors and effectively filters out mold spores and other contaminants. They can be reactivated by placing them in the sun for about an hour once a month. They can be used as an alternative to baking soda air fresheners and are much healthier than traditional air fresheners.

DIFFUSER

Diffusers are devices that are used to dispense essential oils into the air. This can be a great way to disperse the scent of essential oils throughout your home eliminating the need for toxic air fresheners.

FUNNEL

A funnel is not completely necessary, but a useful tool for pouring liquids into the bottles when making the recipes.

LENS/SCREEN MICROFIBER CLOTHS

Lens/screen microfiber cloths are much better to use on screens, small electronics, or glasses than traditional microfiber cloths.

MASON JARS AND GLASS STORAGE CONTAINERS

Mason jars and glass storage containers are great for when you make air fresheners or candles, or for store your cleaning supplies.

MEASURING CUP

Glass is the best thing you can use when measuring and pouring the liquids in the recipes, as glass is non-porous and will not leach any chemicals into the product. But if you do not have a glass measuring cup, any liquid measuring cup is fine to use as nothing will be staying in there for long.

NOTEBOOK

In case you come up with any new recipes, revisions, or ideas not listed in this book, it is a great idea to write them down in a notebook and date them. Trust me, they are easy to forget. You can always use digital note taking applications if you prefer.

PET HAIR/LINT REMOVERS

A reusable pet hair/lint remover can be great for cleaning lint and pet hair off furniture, drapes, bedding, and clothes, and it is much more economical than its disposable counterparts.

PROTECTIVE EYE-WEAR

Protective eye-wear is a must-have if working with hydrogen peroxide at levels higher than 3% or sodium percarbonate that is not highly diluted.

PUMICE STONE/SCOURING STICK

When you have toilet rings that just won't budge, instead of resorting to chemical cleaners, use a pumice stone to make them disappear. These work great on any porcelain surfaces. Make sure to wet the stone before using it, so it does not damage the surface. A pumice stone can also be used to clean the inside of an oven and clean cook-top grates.

SCRAPER

When the abrasives just won't do the job, a scraper is the tool to use. A scraper can be great for attacking sticky residue or built up soap scum.

SIFTER OR STRAINER

A small mesh sifter or strainer is handy to sift baking soda over carpet and mattresses.

SMALL SQUEEGEE

A small squeegee comes in handy for cleaning shower walls and doors as well as windows. It can also help remove embedded pet hair from carpet and upholstery.

STEAMERS

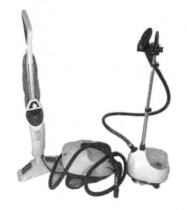

I mention steam cleaners as optional cleaning methods in this book. They are green because they clean and disinfect with pure, hot water. The ones I personally use include a clothes steamer, steam mop and a heavy-duty steamer for deep cleaning. They are not a necessary part of a green cleaning routine, although they can be useful and helpful.

TOOTHBRUSHES

Toothbrushes are great for cleaning smaller areas and grout. If you use an old toothbrush, make sure you run it through the dishwasher before using it for cleaning.

It is important to start making the switch from disposable cleaning tools to reusable ones in as many areas as possible. People tend to overestimate the convenience of these disposable products and they come at a high cost, both in household expenses and how much they contribute to non-recyclable landfill waste. Some of the most common and expensive disposable cleaning tools are floor cleaning pads, lint rollers for pet hair, disposable toilet brushes, sponges, and cleaning wipes. Using disposable versions of these products can end up costing the average family around $250 a year. That is not even including the cost of paper towels. Switching to a reusable version (like microfiber cloths) could save you on average another $200 a year. That could be a $450 annual savings for the average family just by switching to more reusable items. By keeping reusable cleaning tools and the right cleaners and ingredients on hand, the convenience level will still be there, but with a lower cost to the environment and your bank account.

References mentioned in the preceding text box may be found at endnotes 38 and 39.[38][39]

CHAPTER 3. NOTES ON ESSENTIAL OILS

I wish I learned about essential oils earlier in life. Essential oils are distilled or pressed plant matter where the healing and protective essences of the plants are pulled from the original plant matter to create a potent, volatile oil. They are nature's original pharmaceuticals; referenced in the bible, used by Cleopatra, ancient cultures, and kings throughout history for their healing, disinfecting, and beautifying properties.

Essential oils, by nature, are antibacterial in a way that still supports healthy bacterial balance, antifungal, and antimicrobial, which is why they are a great ingredient in making cleaning supplies. They are also multi-purpose and can be used for more than just cleaning, such as in aromatherapy applications, DIY personal care products, and health remedies.

Essential oils are also serious business. Just one drop of essential oil is equivalent to 15-40 cups of medicinal tea. I highly recommend that you research the safe use of essential oils before using them, but here are some precautions that you should be aware of.

ESSENTIAL OIL CAUTIONS

Not all essential oil brands are created equal. There are not a lot of standards or regulations when it comes to creating, labeling, and distributing essential oils. At TheRevolutionBlog.com/cleaning-resources, I list the essential oil brands I personally recommend and trust. Synthetic oils and fragrance oils are not essential oils and should not be used as such, but many are still labeled as essential oils.

There is always the possibility of having an allergy to specific essential oils. It is important you do a patch test on your skin, using some carrier oil mixed with the essential oil you are going to use, to make sure you or your family members do not have an allergic reaction to the oils you plan to use. If you already know you are allergic to the plant, don't use the essential oil. Essential oils are highly concentrated and should always be diluted. Most essential oils cannot be applied directly to the skin without the use of a carrier oil like olive, almond, coconut, jojoba, apricot, etc.

Essential oils do not bind that well to water, so it is best for water to always be the last ingredient added when using essential oils to make cleaning products Adding water last allows the other ingredients combine well before it is added.

Certain essential oils should not be used when pregnant or around small children. If you are pregnant or have small kids I list any cautions I am aware of regarding use around small kids or during pregnancy under each oil. However, I always recommend you do your own research on the oils you use to ensure they are safe for your intended circumstances. The oils safe for children which can change based on age, so it's best to confirm what is safe for the age ranges of your children and family.

Be cautious when using essential oils around pets, especially if the essential oil has specific cautions for your pet. If you have cats and dogs in the house, I recommend you limit the use of essential oils on surfaces they are constantly in contact with like floors and furniture, and only use essential oils that are safe for your animals. As mentioned previously, cats can be especially sensitive because of their heightened ability to absorb these types of things through their skin. Dogs can be sensitive to certain essential oils as well. I list any special precautions regarding essential oils and pets if applicable under each essential oil. Please do further research if you are going to be using essential oils around your pets as there is so much conflicting information on what is safe to use which may have a lot to do with the quality of essential oil used.

Essential oils should never be ingested unless they are pure-grade and used as instructed by a qualified practitioner.

Essential oils should be stored in a cool, dark place away from pets and children. Products that contain essential oils should never be stored in plastic. They will start to break down the plastic and some of the components of the plastic will leach into the product. They are also photosensitive, and should be stored in amber, cobalt, or violet glass bottles. The same guidelines apply when making your own products containing essential oils.

Some essential oils, especially most citrus, are phototoxic so be careful if using on skin before going out in the sun.

If you ever get essential oil on your skin or other area and it burns or irritates, do not use water to remove it. Instead, use a carrier oil by applying the carrier oil directly to the affected area.

Essential oils have many benefits when it comes to green cleaning, but it's important to use them safely. There is a lot of misinformation out there when it comes to using them safely and appropriate use cases for them. If you do not feel comfortable using them, don't. Essential oils are not a required ingredient to green clean your home.

ESSENTIAL OILS USED IN THIS BOOK

The essential oils listed below are the ones used in the recipes in this book. Each essential oil listed has many benefits, and it's worth doing your own research to understand their uses and precautions. I mainly put the benefits for the uses in cleaning. I also listed the cautions for each specific oil, but all the essential oils need to be used with caution as outlined above.

These essential oils are a good starting point when it comes to green cleaning. As you become more comfortable with green cleaning and essential oil, feel free to experiment utilizing other essential oils and coming up with your own scent combinations.

For even more information on essential oils, their cleaning benefits and additional precautions for safe use around pets, kids and while pregnant please visit TheRevolutionBlog.com/cleaning-references.

LAVENDER

Lavender essential oil is the most popular essential oil in aromatherapy. It has a calming, relaxing scent many people love. It also has many uses and is good to keep around the house for things like bug bites and burns. It's great to use in cleaning because it has tremendous antibacterial and deodorizing properties. A common use of lavender is to freshen things like laundry, carpets, and upholstery. It helps repel insects and keep moths away from clothes.

Cautions: None specific to lavender oil unless allergic.

LEMON

Lemon essential oil is great for your cleaning arsenal because it is a powerful disinfectant and has a pleasant, clean fragrance, which is why so many cleaners use synthetic versions of lemon oil in their products. It also makes a great insect repellant and spot remover. Lemon essential oil has great degreasing and natural brightening properties. A high-quality lemon essential oil is an oil I would recommend for items that touch food, due to its ability to protect the food against E. coli and salmonella.

PEPPERMINT

Peppermint essential oil is cooling and refreshing. Its best use for cleaning is to help deter pests and insects like spiders, mice, and ants. It is also antibacterial and great for disinfecting.

Cautions: Do not use if you are pregnant, breastfeeding, have epilepsy, or around small children due to its stimulating effects and high menthol content. Be cautious about its use around cats and dogs due to the strong smell and properties that could be harmful to them. A great substitute for peppermint is spearmint.

ROSEMARY

Rosemary essential oil has a fresh herbal scent. It is highly antibacterial and disinfecting, which is why it's such a powerhouse when it comes to cleaning. It's great at improving mental clarity, which can be a hidden benefit while cleaning.

Cautions: Do not use if pregnant, breastfeeding, or around small children due to its stimulating effects. It should also be avoided by people with epilepsy or

hypertension. A great substitute for rosemary in the recipes would be spearmint.

Spearmint

Because I listed this as a great substitute oil, I thought I would list it separately even though it is not used in the book. Spearmint has a sweet, minty scent. It is still stimulating and uplifting but less potent than peppermint or rosemary, making it a nice alternative for pregnant women or for use around small children and pets. Spearmint makes an excellent antibacterial and antimicrobial cleaner and combines well with lavender making it a great substitute for rosemary in the **Rosemary Lavender Cleaner**. It is also a great natural insecticide for deterring ants and spiders.

Cautions: None specific to spearmint unless allergic.

Sweet Orange

There are a few different types of orange essential oil, but the one I list in this book is cold-pressed sweet orange. Sweet orange has a wonderful, uplifting fragrance and is also an excellent disinfectant and degreaser. Sweet orange is great at removing sticky messes and cleaning/conditioning wood.

Cautions: Use caution when using around cats. Do not use on any area cats are regularly in contact with or would lick or rub as cats are highly sensitive to most citrus oils.

TEA TREE

Tea tree oil has a medicinal aroma, so it may not appeal to everyone. It's predominantly used in cleaning for its powerful antibacterial, antiseptic, and antifungal properties. Besides just being a great disinfectant, it can help fight mold, mildew, and fungus.

Cautions: Be cautious about using tea tree oil around cats and dogs due to the strong smell and properties that can be harmful to them. Also, be more cautious about its use if pregnant or around small children. Do your research as there is a lot of conflicting information when it comes to the safe use of tea tree essential oil. It is a very strong oil. Always err on the side of caution.

Chapter 4. Recipes

Rosemary Lavender All-Purpose Cleaner

This cleaner is my all-star all-purpose cleaner as it is safe and effective for so many surfaces and has an amazing scent. It is my go-to glass and surface cleaner. It is fantastic for cleaning granite, quartz, and other natural stone counter-tops! Can also be used to clean windows, mirrors, stainless steel, varnished wood, and basically any surface you can think of.

You will need:

$1/2$ cup vodka

1 $1/4$ cup distilled water

6 drops rosemary essential oil

6 drops lavender essential oil

5 drops grapefruit seed extract (optional)

16 oz. amber or cobalt glass spray bottle

Add all ingredients to the spray bottle, adding the water last. Shake well.

 K.I.S.S. Add 1 part vodka to 3 parts distilled water in a plastic spray bottle. Shake well.

CITRUS VINEGAR ALL-PURPOSE CLEANER

This is another great all-purpose cleaner that serves all the purposes as the Rosemary Lavender Cleaner, but it cannot be used on granite, marble, or other natural stone surfaces. It is a great disinfectant, and the lemon version can also double as a produce wash as both lemon essential oil and grapefruit seed extract along with vinegar are good for washing fruits and veggies.

YOU WILL NEED:

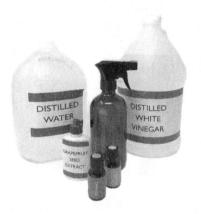

$^1/_2$ cup distilled white vinegar

1 $^1/_4$ cup distilled water

16 drops lemon or sweet orange essential oil

5 drops grapefruit seed extract (optional)

16 oz. amber or cobalt glass spray bottle

Add all ingredients to the spray bottle, adding water last. Shake well.

 K.I.S.S. Add 1 part vinegar to 3 parts distilled water in a plastic spray bottle. Shake well.

3% HYDROGEN PEROXIDE CLEANER

Hydrogen peroxide can serve as a non-toxic alternative for anything you used chlorine bleach for. It is a powerful disinfectant and a multi-purpose cleaner that you can use for all the same situations as the Rosemary Lavender Cleaner and the Citrus Vinegar Cleaner, which can also be used on granite/natural stone and as a produce wash. Keep this mixture away from silver and copper as it will cause them to oxidize. When I reference using hydrogen peroxide in this book, I am always talking about the 3% diluted version, which I show you how to make in this book. You will save money by purchasing the 35% food grade version and diluting it yourself.

YOU WILL NEED:

Protective eye-wear

Gloves

$^1/_4$ cup + 1 tbsp. 35% hydrogen peroxide

3 $^1/_2$ cups + 3 tbsp. distilled water

32 oz. opaque plastic spray bottle (I recommend purchasing a 32-oz. bottle of pre-diluted food grade hydrogen peroxide first. It comes in a white plastic opaque container. Add a spray nozzle and it is reusable to make your own once it runs out)

**Be very careful when working with 35% hydrogen peroxide as it is caustic. Use the protective eye-wear and gloves when you pour everything into the spray bottle. Close the bottle tightly, and shake well.

 K.I.S.S. Just buy a bottle of 3% drug store hydrogen peroxide or pre-diluted 3% food grade hydrogen peroxide and add a spray nozzle.

HOMEMADE SOFT SCRUB

      This homemade soft scrub recipe can be used on any surface where you need something more abrasive. I recommend making it in small batches each time you need it as it will not store well. This works well with microfiber cloths or scouring pads to get tough stains off solid surfaces as well as disinfecting them. Simply rub the scrub on the dirty surface and then rinse or wipe away with cool water or vinegar cleaner. If heavier degreasing is needed, you can let it sit anywhere from a few to 20 minutes.

YOU WILL NEED:

    3% hydrogen peroxide cleaner

    Baking soda

    Castile soap

    Small glass container

    A few drops of lemon or tea tree essential oil (optional)

Mix equal parts baking soda and Castile soap. Add a little 3% hydrogen peroxide in a small container in the amount you need, and add essential oils if using. You can also add table salt if more abrasion is needed. You can also apply these ingredients directly to the surface. If you don't use essential oil, there is no need to premix.

    K.I.S.S. Make a simple paste of baking soda and 3% hydrogen peroxide or baking soda and Castile soap (can also substitute any ecological dish soap in the place of the Castile soap).

For a simple scouring powder just use baking soda or a mixture of baking soda and salt. You can also add some lemon essential oil for a scent boost.

LIQUID DISH SOAP

YOU WILL NEED:

$^3/_4$ cup Castile soap

$^1/_2$ cup distilled water

$^1/_4$ cup vinegar

20 drops sweet orange essential oil

5 drops grapefruit seed extract (optional)

Glass pump soap dispenser

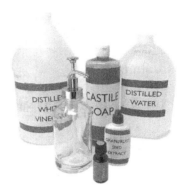

Combine all ingredients in the glass pump soap dispenser. Shake well.

K.I.S.S. Pour Castile soap into the glass pump soap dispenser until it's half full. Fill the rest of the way with distilled water. You could also add a splash of vinegar if you choose. Shake well.

Note about combining vinegar with castile soap: They don't combine well so you will notice some separation in this product. That's fine, it doesn't change the effectiveness of the ingredients. The reason I add vinegar is because I experimented with several DIY liquid dish soap recipes and this is the one I liked best. Vinegar helps the dishes rinse cleaner and helps with hard water. This product will not bubble and suds like more conventional liquid dish soap, but I assure you it is still doing its job getting your dishes effectively and safely clean.

MOISTURIZING HAND SOAP

YOU WILL NEED:

Castile soap

Distilled water

2 tbsp. almond oil

15 drops lavender essential oil

10 drops rosemary essential oil

7 drops tea tree essential oil (optional)

1 tbsp. vegetable glycerin (optional)

5 drops grapefruit seed extract (optional)

Glass pump soap dispenser (use a foaming soap dispenser for an extra luxurious hand soap, or for a thicker consistency).

Pour Castile soap into the glass pump soap dispenser until it's about one-third full. Add the other ingredients and fill the rest of the dispenser with distilled water. Shake well. This hand soap will not be as thick as more traditional hand soaps but it works very well and is much safer and more beneficial to use.

For a version safe for young children, either substitute the rosemary for spearmint or just use orange essential oil in the mix. It is a very kid safe essential oil and kids tend to love the smell.

 K.I.S.S. Pour Castile soap into the glass pump soap dispenser until it's one-third full. Fill the rest of the dispenser with distilled water. Shake well.

ELECTRONIC CLEANER

This basic Electronic Cleaner is great for cleaning small electronics, computers, cell phones, and even eyeglasses. I recommend you use a small microfiber cloth meant for use on electronics when using this cleaner on more delicate surfaces. For electronics, it is important to always spray the cloth and use the cloth to clean instead of spraying the electronics directly. It also works well as a simple disinfecting spray.

YOU WILL NEED:

   1 part vodka

   1 part distilled water

   8 oz. plastic or glass mister bottle

Fill the bottle with equal parts vodka and distilled water. Shake well.

STAIN REMOVER

This stain remover can be used on carpet, clothing, and fabric alike, but be sure to do a small test area first to make sure it does not fade the fabric. This is not something that will store well so just make enough for one application at a time. Hydrogen peroxide works best on lighter fabrics. *For dark or brightly colored fabrics use a simple mixture of one part each vinegar and water to pre-treat the stain along with Castile soap instead of Hydrogen peroxide.* Castile soap can be replaced with an ecologically simple dish soap in this recipe as well.

YOU WILL NEED:

3% Hydrogen Peroxide Cleaner

Castile soap

Small glass container

Mix equal parts hydrogen peroxide and Castile soap in a small container in the amount you need as it will not keep well. For larger areas and stains, dilute the solution with some water. You do not need to premix you can also just apply both ingredients directly to the stain.

 K.I.S.S. Just rub in a little Castile or dish soap directly on the stain. Or on lighter fabrics just spray a little hydrogen peroxide.

Mold and Mildew Remover

This is a strong spray that can be used to kill mold and mildew. Apply directly to the area and let sit for ten or more minutes before removing with a hot damp cloth. Repeat as needed.

You will need:

1 cup distilled white vinegar

Distilled water

40 drops tea tree essential oil

16 oz. glass amber or cobalt spray bottle

Add all ingredients to spray bottle, adding water last and filling to the top. Shake well.

LINEN SPRAY/AIR FRESHENER

This spray is a great spray air freshener alternative to freshen rooms or linens. Another great way to dispense it into a room is to use a diffuser with essential oils. Conventional air fresheners are something I highly recommend you get out of your house. Most of them contain phthalates, which are known to disrupt hormones and can cause other health issues.

YOU WILL NEED:

1 part vodka

2 parts distilled water

1/4 teaspoon vegetable glycerin (optional)

4 oz. cobalt glass mister bottle

20 drops essential oils of choice (lavender or orange work very well but get creative here and mix and match essential oils of your choice)

Fill the bottle to the half-way mark with vodka. Add the essential oils and glycerin if using. Add distilled water to fill the rest of the bottle.

FABRIC REFRESHER

This can be used in place of traditional fabric refreshers to spray on clothes and upholstered furniture to absorb odors.

YOU WILL NEED:

1 cup vodka

1 cup white vinegar

2 tsp. cornstarch (optional)

20 drops essential oils of choice (optional)

16 oz. cobalt or amber glass spray bottle if using essential oil. A plastic spray bottle is fine if not using essential oil.

Pour all ingredients into the spray bottle. Shake well.

 K.I.S.S. Just use a spray bottle filled with straight vodka as a fabric refresher.

BAKING SODA AIR FRESHENERS

These can be great to keep in closets, drawers, the fridge (with just plain baking soda), or anywhere you want to eliminate odors. Lavender and cedar chips can be great to repel bugs like moths and are good to use in closets and drawers that hold your clothes. Plain baking soda works best in areas like the refrigerator where you do not want competing smells. Charcoal air filters also work well in the fridge and other areas of the home.

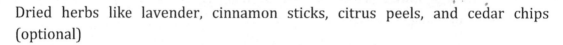

YOU WILL NEED:

Baking soda

8-15 drops essential oils of choice

Dried herbs like lavender, cinnamon sticks, citrus peels, and cedar chips (optional)

Small mason jar with holes poked in the top or muslin bags with a drawstring or ribbon to tie shut. You can purchase small, unbleached muslin bags where loose-leaf tea is sold or at many health food stores.

Fill your container of choice partially with baking soda then add herbs and essential oils of choice. Some of my favorite herb essential oil combinations are lavender herbs with peppermint or spearmint essential oil; and cedar chips with sweet orange essential oil, but you can use any combination you choose. These should last approximately one to three months before needing to be emptied and refilled.

 K.I.S.S. Just use plain baking soda in the mason jar or muslin bag.

GUNK REMOVER

This is a natural alternative to some of the pricier goo removers and can be used to remove stickers and other gooey messes on glass and hard surfaces. This product will not keep well so just make the amount needed for one application at a time. To use, apply to spot, wait about ten minutes, and then wipe clean with warm water.

YOU WILL NEED:

Baking soda

Coconut oil

Few drops of sweet orange essential oil (optional)

Small glass container

Mix equal parts baking soda and coconut oil in the glass container and add essential oil. Mix well. (Not to be used on most fabrics as the coconut oil may stain the fabric.) Can be followed up with a vinegar spray to help get the extra residue off.

FURNITURE POLISH

This furniture polish is to be used on varnished wood surfaces when some extra shine is needed, not on unfinished wood surfaces. Only make a small amount because it will not keep long.

YOU WILL NEED:

1 tbsp. olive oil or sweet almond oil

3 tbsp. white vinegar

3 drops of lemon or orange essential oil (optional)

Small plastic or glass mister bottle

Mix all ingredients in the bottle. Shake well.

MATTRESS CLEANER/CARPET DEODORIZER

This recipe is great to clean mattresses and deodorize carpets. Feel free to use the essential oils you prefer, but I recommend if you have dogs, cats, or crawling babies not to use essential oils in the carpet deodorizer or be very careful of the ones you use to make sure they are safe for your animals and children.

YOU WILL NEED:

1 cup baking soda

10 drops essential oil (optional)

Small glass mixing container

Sifter

Combine ingredients in a small glass container. Pour into a sifter and sift onto the desired area. Let the deodorizer/cleaner set for 30 minutes, then vacuum up.

 K.I.S.S. Just use plain baking soda to sprinkle on carpets or mattresses.

PEST REPELLANT HOUSE SPRAY

Use this spray around windows, exterior doors, etc. to keep pests away.

YOU WILL NEED:

1 cup distilled white vinegar

Distilled water

16 oz. glass amber or cobalt spray bottle

5 drops each of tea tree, peppermint, rosemary, and lavender essential oil

Add all ingredients to the spray bottle, adding water last to fill to the top. Shake well.

Non-Toxic, Air Cleaning Candles

Not only are these candles non-toxic, but according to some sources, they help clean the air as they burn. I recommend using 4-ounce mason jars to make these, but you can use any glass or ceramic container you choose. Vintage teacups can be a very cute option as well. Beeswax candles have a nice, slight honey smell, and I recommend you leave them unscented. You can add essential oils if you choose, but I personally prefer to scent a room using essential oils with a diffuser instead of a candle.

YOU WILL NEED:

1 cup beeswax

$1/2$ cup coconut oil

100% pure cotton wicks size 4

Metal melting/pouring pitcher

Pot with water

Stove

2-3 4 oz. Mason jars

Pencil or bobby pin to secure wick

Start by melting the beeswax using the double boiler method: place the metal pitcher in a pot of water on the stove-top over medium-low heat. Once the beeswax is melted, add the coconut oil, and stir together. In the meantime, secure your wicks with a bobby pin or by wrapping around a pencil so they stay taut in the jar. Pour in the beeswax and let sit until hardened, which usually takes about 15 minutes. Trim the wick to about $1/4$ inch. Let the beeswax candle cure for 48 hours before lighting.

CHAPTER 5. CLEANING DIFFERENT AREAS USING NATURAL PRODUCTS

HOW TO DISINFECT SURFACES WHEN GREEN CLEANING YOUR HOME

Any disinfectants, conventional or green, need to sit on a surface for some length of time to kill all the germs and bacteria. The only exception is a strong concentration of chlorine bleach or 35% food grade hydrogen peroxide. Both can kill germs in about 20 seconds but are dangerous to use at such high concentrations.

The difference between green disinfectants and conventional disinfectants is green disinfectants do not need to be rinsed off once they have finished the disinfecting process, as they are not hazardous to your health, in the same way, that a lot of conventional disinfectants are.

It seems, when people switch over to green cleaning, they are concerned that green cleaning products won't disinfect and clean as well as the commercial products they previously purchased. That is not the case. Diluted hydrogen peroxide has a similar disinfecting result as diluted chlorine bleach. The solutions being diluted makes them safer to use, but again, they need sit on the surface longer to have the same effect they would have if being used in a higher concentration. A lot of the ingredients used in this book, like hydrogen peroxide, vinegar, and vodka, are very strong disinfectants. Most people are already fully aware of the disinfecting properties in alcohol by its use in first aid kits. Hydrogen peroxide is even approved by many hospitals for sterilization. Some of the bonus ingredients we add to the cleaners also have many disinfecting properties, like essential oils and grapefruit seed extract, which adds antimicrobial, antibacterial, and antifungal benefits to the products.

I love to use the **Electronic Cleaner** recipe, which is about 50% alcohol, to regularly disinfect surfaces like cell phones and other small electronics.

The **Electronic Cleaner** is also great for doorknobs, handles, light switches, remote controls, handrails, or anything else with high hand traffic. Just spray on a cloth then wipe down the object.

3% Hydrogen Peroxide Cleaner can be used like chlorine bleach when it comes to being a disinfectant. It works on all those surfaces just listed as well, but I like to use it primarily for disinfecting toilets, bathtubs, showers, and floors.

A powerful way to disinfect and get rid of virtually every germ and bad bacteria is to spray surfaces with both the **3% Hydrogen Peroxide Cleaner** and the **Citrus Vinegar Cleaner** or other vinegar-based cleaner. Let it sit for 10-20 minutes before spraying again and wiping down. It is **very important never to combine the hydrogen peroxide and vinegar in a closed container before use** as it creates Peracetic acid when combined in a container but spraying them one after another does not have the same effect and is a safe way to combine these two ingredients

A study run by Dr. Susan Sumber, Ph.D. at Virginia Polytechnic Institute and State University, found that pairing the two in this fashion worked exceptionally well in sanitizing counter-tops and other food preparation surfaces. The combination kills virtually all Salmonella and E. coli along with other bacteria, proving the effectiveness of hydrogen peroxide and vinegar in combination as disinfectants rendering more common commercial disinfectants like chlorine bleach unnecessary for this effect.[40]

I find this disinfecting method works best on sinks, food preparation surfaces and counter-tops not made of natural stone. It can also be used to disinfect bathtubs, shower stalls, and toilets. Keep in mind to only use this method on vinegar-safe surfaces and not on anything made with natural stone. Use the **3% Hydrogen Peroxide Cleaner** for extra disinfecting on those types of surfaces if needed, otherwise any alcohol based cleaner like the **Rosemary Lavender Cleaner** works well at disinfecting those surfaces.

Another issue is using the sponge or dirty dishrag to clean counters and kitchens. The kitchen may appear clean because it is constantly wiped down with a sponge or a dirty dishrag. But sponges and dirty dishrags can harbor countless germs and bacteria. With this being such a common and widely accepted cleaning method, there may be some reluctance to change. However, bacteria can be very dangerous to your health and has become more resistant to antibiotics, so it is worthwhile to learn the right cleaning practices and make sure the supplies you clean with are clean and sanitary.

BATHROOM

BATHTUBS

Spray bathtub with the **3% Hydrogen Peroxide Cleaner**, let it sit for 10 or more minutes, spray again then sprinkle some baking soda and squirt some Castile soap or use the **Homemade Soft Scrub** to give it a good scrub with a microfiber cloth or scouring pad. Finally rinse with cold water.

Are you bathing in chemical soup?

All the products I mention here to clean your bathtub are completely safe to bathe in even without being rinsed off beforehand. Each one of them can also be considered a helpful bath additive for a variety of conditions. On the other hand, bathing in hot water in a bathtub that has been cleaned with conventional cleaners will open your pores to allow these toxic chemicals for easier absorption into your body. How's that for relaxing?

When cleaning showers and bathtubs, I like to start by using a small square of a damp paper towel to wipe up any hair I find before cleaning with a microfiber cloth.

To clean shower walls and floors, spray first with any of the all-purpose cleaners then let sit. If there is scum build-up, you can use the **Homemade Soft Scrub** and a scrubber or microfiber cloth, then rinse well. A scraper tool also works well to combat soap scum. When you are done, dry the walls with another microfiber cloth or a squeegee. If you don't have soap scum or other buildup, you can get away with spraying the surface with one of the multi-purpose cleaners followed by a squeegee or wiping with microfiber cloth to keep it clean. If you suspect mold or mildew in your shower, spray it down with the **Mold and Mildew Remover.** Let it sit for ten or more minutes, then wipe down with a hot cloth.

When I want to give my bathroom an especially deep cleaning, I like to use a steam cleaner, which uses just hot water to clean. It is a great, high-powered addition to a green cleaning routine, but not a necessary one.

If you have a shower curtain, it is best to use a cloth liner that you can throw in the washer once a month and wash in hot water with some sodium percarbonate or **3% Hydrogen Peroxide Cleaner.**

Avoid vinyl PVC shower curtains. They contain a high level of VOCs, phthalates, and other toxic compounds that can easily be released into the air and breathed in when taking hot showers.

To clean glass shower doors, use any of the multi-purpose cleaners and either a microfiber cloth or a squeegee.

For everyday shower cleaning, spray down the shower with any of the multi-purpose cleaners and squeegee off or wipe down with a microfiber towel. You can also just spray and let it sit if you don't have glass and therefore do not need to worry about streaks.

TOILETS

To deep clean a toilet, spray the inside of the bowl with the **3% Hydrogen Peroxide Cleaner** and sprinkle in some baking soda. You can add a couple drops of tea tree or peppermint essential oil (optional) by putting it directly in the toilet bowl. Let it sit while you spray down the seat and outside of the toilet and wipe it down with a clean paper towel. Then, add some vinegar to your toilet bowl, and while foaming, scrub the bowl with a toilet brush. Once scrubbed, flush the toilet, rinse the brush in the clean toilet water, spray the toilet brush with **3% Hydrogen Peroxide Cleaner** and put it under the toilet lid to hang dry. For extra disinfecting let the cleaner sit on the toilet for 10-20min before wiping the toilet down with a paper towel.

For a quick cleaning of the toilet, spray any of the multi-purpose cleaners inside the bowl, do a quick scrub with the brush and a quick wipe-down of the outside with the same cleaner and a paper towel.

For stubborn toilet rings use a pumice stone or scouring stick but make sure to wet it first so it does not scratch the porcelain.

> Ladies and Gentlemen, make sure you put the entire toilet lid down before you flush. It is not just a myth that germs are spread when the toilet is flushed. In fact, Mythbusters did an investigation and confirmed there is, in fact, fecal matter on toothbrushes caused from flushing the toilet with the lid open because the mist from flushing the toilet can travel up to 15 feet in the air, covering most, if not all, your bathroom surfaces meaning your toothbrush is not the only thing fecal matter gets on.
>
> This is a call for all genders to put the toilet seat down!

References mentioned in the preceding text box may be found at endnote 41.[41]

COUNTER-TOP/SINK

For everyday counter-top and sink cleaning, use any multi-purpose cleaner appropriate for the counter type. Spray the counters and sink, then wipe clean with a microfiber towel. When extra disinfecting is needed, use the vinegar and 3% hydrogen peroxide method previously described if it is safe for your counter surface. My favorite counter-top cleaner for stone counters like granite and quartz is the **Rosemary Lavender Cleaner**.

When you have extra grime that has built up, use the **Homemade Soft Scrub** with a cloth or scouring pad to give a deep cleaning. This method works best on sinks and non-stone counter-tops, as you must be very careful with the level of abrasion you use on granite or other stone surfaces like quartz. It will, however, make your kitchen sink shine!

DOING DISHES

Let's talk dirty: the kitchen sponge is by far the dirtiest thing in your house and 200,000 times dirtier than your toilet seat.[42] In a study published in a scientific journal they found 362 different species of bacteria living on kitchen sponges. The density of the bacteria was astounding and reached up to 45 billion per square centimeter.[43] This includes very dangerous bacteria like E. coli, Salmonella, and Staphylococcus. Cellulose sponges provide the perfect habitat for bacteria to cling to and stay alive and cannot be properly sanitized according to the same study. The funny thing to me is that sponges are most commonly used to wash dishes used for food! This is why you do not see sponges anywhere on my recommended cleaning tools. I have not personally used them in years, and I haven't missed them in the slightest.

I highly recommend you ditch the dirty sponges and start using dish brushes when doing dishes. They do the dishes better, do not harbor germs and bacteria the way sponges do, and are easily cleaned and disinfected by either spraying them down with the **3% Hydrogen Peroxide Cleaner** between uses or running them through the dishwasher.

You can easily hand wash items using the **Liquid Dish Soap** recipe and a dish brush.

You will notice that I do not have dishwasher detergent listed as a recipe in this book. That is because I could not find anything I liked to use that was simple and had ingredients I prefer while still working well. This is an area where it is important to have enzymes and is the one cleaning product I still purchase. I list what I currently use at **TheRevolutionBlog.com/cleaning-resources**. Just be sure whatever you purchase is natural, has enzymes, and is phosphate free.

In your dishwasher, you can use distilled white vinegar as the rinse aid to get rid of water spots instead of using a commercial rinse aid. If you are worried about using vinegar in the rinse aid compartment due to its acidity, you can just pour it into a glass and set on the top shelf before running the load along with your other dishes. For a vinegar-free option, you can try using hydrogen peroxide as your rinse aid. If hard water is a problem for you and you do not already have a water softener I recommend looking into dishwasher salts which are a special form of salt that are safe to use in dishwashers.

When it comes to doing dishes, you eat off them, so the last thing you want to do is be cleaning them with toxic chemicals when there are so many natural and safer alternatives.

CAST IRON SKILLET

Many health-conscious people use a cast iron skillet, which must be hand washed. You are not supposed to use soap on cast iron cookware.

If there is food stuck on the skillet, sprinkle salt on the bottom, add a little hot water, and scrub with a nylon dish brush. The dish brush will probably turn black, so it is not a bad idea to have one specifically for your cast iron cookware. Another way to clean your skillet is to heat it up on the stove with some salt and water while using a wooden spatula (not plastic) to scrape food off the bottom. Otherwise, if there is no stuck-on food, simply rinse the pan with very hot water and dry thoroughly. While the pan is still hot, but cool enough to touch, use a cloth or paper towel to add a thin coat of coconut oil. Store without the lids, and if stacking, layer with cloths or paper towels.

If your cast iron is in bad shape, needs some restoration, or is rusted, do a more intense cleaning with dish soap and steel wool, then season it right afterward.

SEASONING CAST IRON

To season a cast iron skillet, coat it with coconut oil and bake it in the oven at 400 degrees for one hour with the pan upside down on the oven rack. You may want to put a drip pan on the bottom of the oven to catch drips. Also, use the stove fan, as there is a chance of smoke. Once seasoned, do not use soap or steel wool unless you need to restore it again and remove the previous seasoning.

Vitamix Blender

I know you are probably wondering why I am putting specific instructions on how to clean a Vitamix Blender. It's because a lot of health-conscious people either have one or want one. They are not dishwasher safe and difficult to keep clean as the container gets cloudy easily due to mineral build up. Of course, these cleaning instructions would work for any blender container that is not dishwasher safe.

Fill the container with hot water until it is $^3/_4$ full and sprinkle in baking soda. Put the lid on and blend for approximately 30-60 seconds. Take off the lid and scrub the inside of the container and lid with a nylon scrub brush. Pour out the baking soda solution. Next, fill the container $^3/_4$ full of cold water and pour in some vinegar. Blend again with the lid on for approximately 30-60 seconds. Pour out the solution, rinse with cold water, and air dry. I do not recommend using dish soap for your Vitamix as it seems to make the cloudy problem worse.

I only do this method about once a week or when I make something in my Vitamix that is on the messier side like soup or nut butter. Most of the time I just make smoothies and rinse the pitcher with hot water between uses. Occasionally, I also like to spray down the inside of it and the tamper with the **3% Food Grade Hydrogen Peroxide Cleaner** and just let it air dry to disinfect. Only do this if you are using the food grade version of the cleaner.

For an extra dirty blender with lots of mineral build up, let the vinegar solution sit overnight. In place of the vinegar, you could blend a whole lemon in water and let that sit overnight. For best results, make sure the liquid inside fills to the top. If the blade accumulates buildup, you can use a scouring pad, but I do not recommend using a scouring pad on the plastic container. It is also a good idea to give the base a wipe down and remove the rubber pad on the base so you can clean anything under it before replacing.

Wood Cutting Board

Always rinse and dry your wood cutting board immediately after use. To get rid of stains, rub some lemon and salt on them. You can spray the **3% Hydrogen Peroxide Cleaner** and the **Citrus Vinegar Cleaner** on them to disinfect and deodorize. Condition your wood cutting board by rubbing it with coconut oil and letting it sit for a few hours. Do not use other natural oils as they can go rancid.

Drains

To keep drains clean, do this tip at least a few times a month: Pour baking soda, then vinegar down the drain. It should begin to foam. Let it sit for five to ten minutes, then follow with boiling water.

Doing this regularly keeps drains from becoming clogged. For more stubborn drains with lots of buildup, you can try one of the following environmentally friendly methods: use salt instead of baking soda for stronger abrasion, use a metal wire hook fashioned out of a metal hanger to remove hair, use a natural enzymatic drain cleaner, snake the drain, use a plunger, or use a drain cleaning tool.

It's never a bad idea to prevent clogged drains with drain protectors or drain protectors. If anyone using your shower has long hair, a hair catcher will prevent clogs and make cleaning easier.

Just be sure to never use a commercial drain cleaner. Not only are they horrible for the environment, but they will also wreak havoc on your pipes.

Do not combine baking soda and vinegar except when foaming action is needed. The two react and neutralize each other when used together, so unless foaming action is needed like in cleaning the toilet or drain, they are best not combined but can be used one after the other.

DUSTING

I do not understand or recommend dry dusting unless it is for very delicate surfaces or hard to reach areas. Dry dusting does not actually get rid of the dust but just moves it around to a different location in the room. Your household dust usually contains flame retardants and other toxic chemicals so the last thing you want it to have it flying around in the air again.

A lot of dusting can be completed with only a microfiber cloth and some water. To add some disinfecting power, you can use any of the multi-purpose cleaners. My favorite is the **Rosemary Lavender Cleaner** with the microfiber cloth.

If you tend to polish your wood furniture when you dust, buff on the **Furniture Polish** from the recipe section in this book in place of your regular furniture polish.

ELECTRONICS

It is a good idea to consult your user manual before cleaning your electronics. This method, however, should be safe for most, if not all of them. Start by making sure the device is shut down and completely turned off. Spray the **Electronic Cleaner** directly on the microfiber cloth first, then use the cloth to wipe down electronics.

If cleaning a laptop, first unplug all cords. Stop using the expensive, wasteful, and toxic can of air, and instead, use a small makeup or paint brush to dust around the keys. You can also turn your laptop or keyboard over and give it a gentle tap to get crumbs out of the keyboard. To clean, wipe down the screen using distilled water and a microfiber cloth meant for lenses and screens. Directly spray the microfiber cloth with the **Electronic Cleaner** and use it to wipe down the keyboard, exterior, mousepad, and mouse, then buff dry. Do not spray cleaner directly on any part of the computer. If needed, use a cotton swab sprayed wet with the cleaner to do more detailing and then buff dry. This method also works for a desktop computer; just make sure it is shut down and completely turned off first, but you can leave cords attached.

Floor Cleaning

Carpet

The most important thing for carpet care is to vacuum it regularly using a vacuum with high suction and a HEPA filter to keep the air clean as well.

To deodorize carpets, simply sift the **Mattress Cleaner/Carpet Deodorizer** or plain baking soda over the carpet and let it sit for around 10-30 minutes, then vacuum up.

For carpet stains, use the **Stain Remover** recipe located in the recipe section and use a little bit of water to dilute it. After applying to the stain, let it sit, and use a rag with cold water to remove the solution once complete. Test in an inconspicuous area before using on the carpet for the first time. Sometimes this method needs to be applied several times to fully remove the stain, but I have always had great success with it. Make sure any rags or cloths you use to wipe your carpet are white or will not cause the color to transfer.

For some stains, you can also sprinkle baking soda then spray with a vinegar and water solution. Let it foam, then wipe down with a wet rag.

Most stains are best to blot and not rub. For more stain removal guidance, consult the stain removal section of the book for other methods depending on stain type.

If you have a particularly tough stain on your carpet after applying these methods, soak some cloths or rags in hot water. Place the soaked rag over the stain then place your iron using the steam function and an appropriate heat setting that will not burn your carpet over the wet rag and stain for about 20 seconds. Repeat with a clean cloth or a clean section of the cloth until the stain is fully removed.

If you steam clean your own carpets, you can create a solution of four tablespoons **3% Hydrogen Peroxide Cleaner** with one and one-half quarts of very hot water and add to your cleaner. Make sure to carefully read the instructions of your carpet cleaner before using this recipe, and spot test to make sure the product does not damage your carpet. If you hire professionals, make sure they clean using only steam or non-toxic, eco-friendly detergents.

HARD SURFACE FLOORING

Be sure to thoroughly sweep or vacuum any hard surface flooring before cleaning.

The best option to clean your hard surface flooring is to use a flat-head mop with one of the following solutions in a spray bottle. Spray the cleaner on the floor in a fine mist, then mop up in the direction of the grain. If you're planning to store the mixture for a long period of time or if you have hard water, use distilled water. Otherwise, tap water is fine for these cleaners. Shake the mixture well before using.

Another option is to use a steam mop on hard surface floors it works well by cleaning them with pure steam but is not recommended for hardwoods due to moisture.

I am providing multiple recipes for cleaning floors because different solutions work differently depending upon the floor surface and its finish. It is important to test the solution in a small area first, then use the one that works best and is safe for your flooring type. Please note any of the multi-purpose cleaners in this book will work to clean hard surface flooring but because so much is used when cleaning floors it is best to mix a quick bottle of your cleaner of choice when you want to clean your hard surface flooring.

- Mix four parts water to one-part vinegar in a plastic spray bottle. This is great for linoleum and laminate flooring. It's also a popular option for hardwood floors, though some people say it is too acidic for regular use on them.
- Fill a spray bottle with one-part vodka to three parts water. This dries very quickly and prevents streaks. This is great for hardwoods but can be used with other flooring surfaces, such as tile as well.

- Mix three parts water, one-part white vinegar, and one-part vodka in a plastic spray bottle.
- If you would like to polish and add extra shine to your hardwood floors, add two tablespoons of olive or sweet almond oil to any of the above floor cleaning recipes (it becomes a onetime use product once oil is added, as will not keep long).

Other floor cleaning options:

- Mix one tablespoon sodium percarbonate with hot water in a spray bottle (one use product will not keep).
- Fill a spray bottle with water, add two drops Castile soap.

Of course, you can add a few drops of essential oils to any of these cleaning recipes. Just make sure they are kid and pet safe if you have kids or pets and running around. Use a glass bottle for mixing anything you are going to store if using essential oils.

GLASS/WINDOWS/MIRRORS

To clean glass, windows, or mirrors, use any vodka or vinegar based cleaner with a microfiber cloth. Test them out to see which one you prefer for cleaning glass. My favorite is the **Rosemary Lavender Cleaner** or just the simple mix of vinegar and water. Distilled water is best on glass surfaces to prevent streaks caused minerals.

To make a glass-specific cleaner that will guarantee a streak-free shine when there is extra grime. Mix one tablespoon cornstarch with 1/3 cup vodka and 1/3 cup vinegar in a spray bottle. Fill the rest of the way with distilled water. Shake well to combine and shake before each use. Feel free to add essential oils if you would like the extra scent.

When cleaning windows it is a good idea to use a squeegee with the glass cleaner of your choice. Wipe the squeegee blade clean after each pass and use a microfiber cloth to wipe the corners and edges. It is best to clean windows on a cloudy day or when the sun is not hitting them directly. Cleaning windows when the sun is shining on them causes them to streak.

GROUT

The **Homemade Soft Scrub** works great applied with a toothbrush for cleaning grout. Let sit for tougher stains then rinse well once done.

A method to clean unsealed grout is to spray directly with white vinegar, scrub with the toothbrush, then wipe down with a wet rag. If you have grout that looks black spray the Mold and Mildew Remover first and let sit for 20 or more minutes before wiping down with a hot cloth then following with one of the other methods.

KITCHEN

GARBAGE DISPOSAL

To freshen your garbage disposal and prevent odors from forming, put some ice and either a lemon wedge or a few drops of lemon essential oil down your garbage disposal and turn the disposal on while cold water is running until the ice is chopped up. You can follow it with some vinegar for extra disinfecting and deodorizing.

MICROWAVE

Microwave a bowl of water and vinegar with a few drops of lemon essential oil (optional) for one-and-one-half minutes. Once done and the mixture has cooled a little, dip a microfiber cloth in the solution (be careful not to burn yourself) and wipe down the inside of the microwave.

OVEN

To clean your oven in lieu of the self-cleaning feature, start by wiping out any loose debris and removing the oven racks. Make sure your oven is turned off and left off the entire time you are cleaning it.

Make a paste of baking soda and water and apply where needed, focusing on the bottom and door. Let sit for at least four hours or overnight. While it's sitting, clean your oven racks by soaking them in the bathtub. First, put down old towels so they don't scratch the tub. Cover them with just enough hot water and a little bit of Castile or dish soap. Let soak for a minimum of two hours. Use a scouring pad to wipe them down. Everything should wipe off easily.

Once the solution in the oven has been applied for four hours or more, wipe down the interior with a damp rag that you don't mind getting dirty. A non-scratching scouring pad can also be used. Continue to wipe the entire oven to remove all baking soda paste. To get the final baking soda residue off, spray a little vinegar based cleaner to make sure all the residue is removed. Repeat this process until there is no more residue.

Replace your oven racks, and you are done! I think you will be surprised at how clean this gets your oven. You may want to use this method instead of the self-cleaning feature so you don't need to deal with the smell or energy use.

REFRIGERATOR

For small spills, or quickly wiping down food messes, use any of the all-purpose cleaners with the cloth.

For cleaning and disinfecting the whole refrigerator, use the method of disinfecting with one or both the **Citrus Vinegar Cleaner** and **3% Hydrogen Peroxide Cleaner**.

Be sure to put a baking soda sachet or charcoal air freshener in your fridge and freezer to keep it smelling fresh and odor free.

STAINLESS STEEL APPLIANCES

Stainless steel appliances can easily be cleaned with a microfiber cloth and some water, but any of the all-purpose cleaners can be used for stainless steel. To add shine and protect your appliances, you can buff a little bit of oil on the appliance with a microfiber cloth, but be careful not to use too much or it will attract dust, a quarter size amount or less is plenty. Buff dry again with a microfiber cloth when done. When cleaning stainless steel, you get the best results by always rubbing or buffing in the direction of the grain.

STOVE TOP

The **Homemade Soft Scrub** works great at combating burned-on grime on your stove top. Any of the multi-purpose cleaners with a microfiber cloth can give it a good shine.

LAUNDRY

You will notice that I have not provided any official laundry recipes in this book. That is because I just use individual ingredients when doing laundry to keep it easy.

My basic laundry detergent is just 6-8 soap nuts in a muslin or mesh bag that can be reused 6-8 times, then composted. Some sources say you can only use soap nuts in hot water while others say you can use them in hot or cold water. I use them in cold water all the time and they seem to get my laundry just as clean. But if you are concerned about using them in cold water, soak them in some hot water first, before adding them to the washer.

If you do not feel comfortable using soap nuts because you think there is no way a nut (technically, a berry shell) could possibly clean your clothes, then look for a recipe you feel comfortable with online or purchase an eco-friendly, plant-based version with natural enzymes. There are also reusable laundry ball products that are non-toxic. I will list more recommendations on laundry products at **TheRevolutionBlog.com/cleaning-resources.**

Dry cleaning is not only expensive, but commercial dry cleaning is highly toxic. Although I'm not claiming this method completely replaces dry cleaning, it will extend the wear-ability of clothes between dry cleaning visits, and you won't need to use the dry cleaners as frequently. When you must take items to the dry cleaners, I recommend you find an eco-friendly one in your area. The main criterion is that they do not use perchloroethylene (or perc for short). Perc is considered a toxic air pollutant by the EPA, meaning that it's "known or suspected to cause cancer or other serious health effects." Visit **TheRevolutionBlog.com/cleaning-references** for information on finding a more eco-friendly dry cleaner.

How to DIY Dry Clean:

Hang item and remove any lint or hair using a lint brush. Then spray down the item, especially the armpits, with either pure vodka (kills bacteria) or the **Fabric Refresher** spray. For more stubborn armpit smells, repeat a few times, focusing on that area and letting the garment dry completely in-between sprays.

The next step is optional but highly recommended, especially if the items are wrinkled. Steam the garment with a clothes steamer, then leave hanging until completely dry. Of course, always check clothing laundering and care labels before laundering garments. If you have a spot or a stain you can try saturating the spot with the spray then gently blotting to see if that removes it. Handwashing can also be a good alternative to dry cleaning for a lot of garments.

Depending on how often you dry clean, you could be disposing upwards of 300 cheap metal hangers in the trash every year. Metal hangers must be recycled as scrap metal. Another solution is to take them back to your dry cleaners every time you return so they can reuse them. While you are there, ask them nicely if they will also post a sign asking their other customers to do the same. This would be mutually beneficially as it would save them lots of money if all their customers did that. If they say no, maybe it is time to find another dry cleaner.

DRYING

If you can, line-dry your wet laundry on a warm, sunny day. This is the best option as nothing brightens, disinfects, or makes clothes smell as good as the sun does. I personally have bars in my laundry room to hang certain clothes from to air dry. If you use a dryer, make sure the lint trap stays clean to increase the energy efficiency of your dryer and prevent house fires.

When using the dryer, instead of using dryer sheets, throw in some dryer balls to help soften clothes, dry them faster, and reduce static. If you want the extra scent, you can add a drop of essential oil to each ball or create a dryer sachet using a muslin bag and dried herb like lavender. Just make sure to use a clip or tie a knot at the top so the dried herbs do not leak from the bag. These methods should be good for several loads. You can also just wet a cloth and put a couple of essential oil drops on it, then throw it in the dryer with your wet laundry.

Dryer sheets are very dangerous to dogs and cats. Dryer sheets tend to float around your house and, due to the appealing smell, cats and dogs like to play with them. When they do get ahold of them, it can lead to problems ranging anywhere from skin irritation to serious gastrointestinal distress, pulmonary edema, and kidney failure.

Never rub your pets with dryer sheets no matter what the information on the internet suggests!

FABRIC SOFTENER

For fabric softener, just add distilled white vinegar to the fabric softener dispenser of the washer or in a fabric softener release ball. I do not like my clothes scented, but if you do, you can add a few drops of essential oil to the vinegar. The vinegar smell will not stay on your clothes when they are done washing, but it will soften them, kill bacteria, remove odors, reduce static, reduce color bleeding, extend the life of your clothes, and even help keep your washing machine clean in the process.

For a vinegar-free fabric softener alternative, just use 1 tablespoon to ¼ cup of table salt depending on the load size. You can also add a few drops of essential oil to the salt for added scent.

IRONING

For ironing, it is easy to make a DIY starch spray by mixing two cups distilled water with two tablespoons cornstarch in a spray bottle and shaking well. You can also add a couple of drops of essential oil if you like. If you do, be sure to use a glass spray bottle. Otherwise, a plastic spray bottle is fine for mixing and using spray starch. You will want to clean your iron occasionally when using this solution as it can build up.

LAUNDRY BOOSTERS

I always add a laundry booster when doing laundry. In cold washes, I add about $1/4$ cup of baking soda as a laundry booster. In hot washes, I use $1/8$ cup sodium percarbonate, which can only be used in hot or warm water. An alternative is to use **3% Hydrogen Peroxide Cleaner** and baking soda if you don't have sodium percarbonate or want to use in cold water. Hydrogen peroxide although it can be color safe is best used on lighter fabrics.

MICROFIBER CLOTHS

I upgraded my own microfiber cloth washing routine to conserve as many resources as possible and to keep the microfibers from shedding outside of my washing machine to prevent microfiber pollution.

"Microfiber pollution" is a term I am sure you will become more familiar with in the coming years. Despite the name, this pollution is not just caused by microfiber cloths and towels. It is a problem when washing virtually any synthetic material as the microfibers that shed from the material make it into our waterways. I do not want this to deter you from using microfiber cloths as they reduce a lot of waste and are a huge benefit to green cleaning. Unless you are going to quit buying and washing synthetic items, the problem remains. The solution needs to come from an invention that will keep these fibers from leaving our washing machines. There are some filters or washing bags available right now that help to catch the fibers as they leave your washing machine but more awareness and solutions are needed to solve this problem.

Microfiber Cloth Laundry Instructions: You never want to use bleach, fabric softeners, or chemical detergents when washing microfiber cloths but you can use all the laundry ingredients listed in this book. There is a lot of varying information on water temperature when washing microfiber cloths, I personally only feel comfortable using hot water for complete sanitation, but wash in whatever temperature you feel comfortable with. It is highly recommended to wash them in a laundry bag designed specifically to catch microfibers to keep them from spreading into waterways. The other benefit to using these bags is you can wash multiple cloths for different areas and other materials at the same time. For example, it is not recommended to wash your microfiber cloths with non-microfiber fabrics or your kitchen cloths with your bathroom cloths as they pick up everything around them including debris and lint from other materials. If you use these bags, you can combine multiple items in the same load by utilizing the bags specifically for your microfiber cloths. When doing this, you still want to make sure the bags are not more than half full and that the washing machine is not overly packed full so everything has room to move freely in the machine. When drying microfiber cloths, the best option is to let them air dry. If this is not practical, you can tumble dry them using no or low heat but you will need to remove them from the bags and dry each category separately.

For in-depth instructions on washing microfiber cloths, info on microfiber pollution, the bags that can stop the microfibers from leaving your machine, and other filtration options available visit **TheRevolutionBlog.com/cleaning-references**.

PRE-TREATING STAINS

For pre-treating stains, I use the **Stain Remover** recipe applied directly to the stain and I find it works on most stains. For more information on how to treat different types of stains see the **Stain Removal** section.

WATER TEMPERATURE

Items like socks and underwear should be washed in hot water instead of cold to get fully disinfected. These items can be washed with items like towels which should also be washed in hot water. Hot water washes should be rinsed with cold water. Most other items can and should be washed in cold water to save energy. For sheets and blankets follow the care label to see what temperature they recommend.

WHITENING AND BRIGHTENING

If I need some extra whitening and brightening power, I do a pre-soak with a mixture of $1/2$ cup **3% Hydrogen Peroxide Cleaner** added to cold water. Or, I add $1/4$ cup sodium percarbonate to hot or warm water before running through the regular wash cycle. Double or triple these amounts if more whitening is needed.

For an extra whitening boost, add ¼ to ½ cup lemon juice to the pre-soak.

MATTRESS AND PILLOWS

It is recommended you flip your mattress every three months or at least twice a year, which is a great time to perform a dry mattress cleaning as well.

MATTRESSES

To clean your mattress, strip down and wash all mattress covers and sheets before putting them back on the bed. Spot treat any stains by using the stain removal methods listed in this book. Sift the **Mattress Cleaner/Carpet Deodorizer** mix over the top of your mattress. Let it sit for 30 minutes to one hour and vacuum it up using a clean upholstery attachment. Flip the mattress and do the same to the other side before putting your clean sheets and mattress pad back on your bed.

The essential oil mixture I recommend for mattresses is lavender and peppermint as it will help deter pests like spiders and bedbugs. I usually like to use peppermint on the side that is going to be on the bottom and lavender on the top. Remember to substitute spearmint for the peppermint for a more kid/pet safe version.

You can also mist pure vodka over your mattress lightly to clean and disinfect as it dries quickly.

PILLOWS

You should wash pillows every time you flip your mattress or, at least, a couple times a year. Most pillows can be washed in the washing machine, depending on the material inside your pillow, but be sure to check the manufacturer's instructions. These instructions should apply to most polyester and feather pillows. When washing pillows in a top load washer, you will want to make sure to put two in at once to balance out the load.

Wash the pillows using warm water, soap nuts, and $1/8$ cup sodium percarbonate or $1/2$ cup **3% Hydrogen Peroxide Cleaner** and baking soda. Once washed, run through a second spin cycle to remove excess water, then pop the pillows into the dryer on a mid-to-low setting with the dryer balls.

Make sure pillows are completely dry by holding them up to your nose and taking a deep breath to make sure there is no moisture left on the pillow. If not completely dry, run through the dryer again until they are completely dry. Once the pillows have been dried for a bit in the dryer to evenly disperse the filling inside, you can hang them on the clothesline as an alternative to finish drying and soak up some fresh sunshine for disinfecting and smelling fresh.

PET HAIR REMOVAL

To remove pet hair, use a reusable pet hair remover mitt or the pet hair attachment on your vacuum cleaner. You can also use a small squeegee to remove embedded pet hair from carpet and upholstery.

STAIN REMOVAL

The **Stain Remover** recipe works great on a variety of stains and fabric types. It is always good to apply to stains as a pre-treatment, then work in with a cleaning toothbrush if needed (although most stains should be blotted instead of rubbed). Let it sit before laundering or rinsing. There are other natural stain removal methods that work best for the following stains. Make sure to spot test in an inconspicuous area, first, to make sure it will not fade the fabric.

INK, MARKER, MAKEUP, AND PAINT STAINS

Apply vodka to stain and let sit for 10-30 minutes before washing or rinsing.

GREASE OR OIL STAINS

Sprinkle with baking soda or cornstarch, then apply with Castile or dish soap before washing or rinsing.

RED WINE STAINS

Blot as much as you can, then saturate the stain with vinegar. Apply the **Stain Remover** recipe without rubbing, before laundering or rinsing with hot water. For carpets, you can also try saturating the area with salt until the stain is covered. Let sit until the salt is dry, then vacuum up.

TOMATO-BASED STAINS

Pour white vinegar directly on the stain, then wash or rinse immediately.

COFFEE AND TEA STAINS

Rinse immediately with cold water, then spray with a vinegar and water solution. Apply some Castile or dish soap, blotting frequently before laundering.

GRASS STAINS

Pre-treat with the **Stain Remover**, vinegar and water mixture or a natural enzyme-based liquid laundry detergent before laundering or rinsing. If that does not work, apply vodka to the area and let sit for 10-30 minutes before laundering or rinsing again.

ARMPIT STAINS

Soak in a bowl filled with vinegar and warm water for at least 20 minutes. Then apply a paste of baking soda and 3% Hydrogen Peroxide Cleaner. Let sit before laundering. To help prevent armpit stains in the future, stop using aluminum-based antiperspirants.

PROTEIN-BASED STAINS

This includes blood, vomit, urine etc. Soak first in cold water, then treat the stain with either the **Stain Remover** recipe or an enzyme-based natural liquid laundry detergent before laundering or rinsing. Hydrogen peroxide on its own is also very effective at removing blood.

KEEPING YOUR HOME GREEN AND CLEAN

Here are some other ways to keep your home green and clean!

KEEPING YOUR HOME SMELLING FRESH

I'm not personally that into scented products anymore, but I understand that chemical air fresheners are difficult for some people to give up. So, here are some of my recommendations for keeping your home smelling fresh without filling the air with toxins.

Some of the main things you can do to keep your home smelling fresh and clean are simple things such as opening windows to air out the house, taking the trash out, cleaning your garbage disposal, and cleaning up after your pets regularly. Other suggestions would be keeping charcoal or baking soda air fresheners in and near areas where odors tend to accumulate like near trashcans, litter-boxes, bathrooms, and closets.

Spray down your furniture and linens using the **Linen Spray/Air Freshener** or **Fabric Refresher** spray (Take care when using essential oils on areas where pets or young kids tend to congregate). Keep your carpets deodorized by using the **Mattress Cleaner/Carpet Deodorizer.**

When expecting company or just to keep your home smelling extra good, use a diffuser to diffuse your favorite essential oils (they even have ones that plug in and can be used just like a plug-in air freshener).

Another great option when you want your home to smell extra nice is to make a stove-top potpourri using either a crockpot (does not need to be monitored) or a regular pot on your stove (does need to be monitored). You can use different combinations of dried herbs, fruit peels, and spices to make your own unique combinations. Just put the ingredients with water in the pot, bring to a boil and then reduce to a low simmer. For a crockpot, add ingredients then fill with water one inch from the rim and let simmer with the lid off. Some of my favorite combinations of dried herbs, spices, and fruity peels are lavender and peppermint, orange and cinnamon, rosemary, vanilla, and lemon.

DIY Reed diffusers are another way to give your home a subtle scent. All you need is a small glass or ceramic jar with a small opening. Fill the jar partially with sweet almond oil, a couple of splashes of vodka, and a few drops of the essential oils of your choice then mix thoroughly. Finally, place some reed sticks in the jar to disperse the scent into the air. These can be placed throughout your home and are a great way to maintain a pleasant scent with very little maintenance. Just rotate reeds occasionally and refill as needed.

Most conventional air-fresheners contain VOC's, Formaldehyde, and Phthalates all of which we discussed the toxic and negative effects of in previous chapters. Another popular toxic ingredient in a lot of conventional air fresheners is 1.4 dichlorobenzene. Exposure to this substance can cause headaches, dizziness, swelling around the eyes, nausea, and vomiting. In addition, according to the National Institutes of Health (NIH), the compound may cause "modest reductions in lung function." Does this sound like something you want to spray in your home to be around you and your loved ones?

KEEPING YOUR PETS CLEAN

Keeping your pets clean helps keep your house clean, but you don't want to clean them with toxic chemicals.

The easiest and most effective natural shampoo for dogs and cats is to mix equal parts unscented Castile soap and warm water. Just make enough for what you are going to be using for one pet bath. Do not use anything scented or any essential oils when bathing your pets. Sometimes even pet-safe options can be very irritating to them, and they have no way of letting you know whether they like the scent. Using a grooming tool to de-shed your pet regularly can help keep pet hair off furniture.

When taking care of your dog's waste make sure to use biodegradable bags. For cat owners, the litter box can be a struggle. The best solution to clean the litter box is to use the **3% Hydrogen Peroxide Cleaner** and let it sit for ten or more minutes before wiping it down. Cats do not like the smell of vinegar so it is not good to use for litter boxes. Also, don't use any cleaner with essential oils to clean the litter box.

Other tricks I've learned for keeping the litter box clean, include the following: mix baking soda with litter to help eliminate odor; use cat litter mats to keep the cat from tracking the litter around the house, and use a Litter Genie to make scooping easy. It is important to use natural and fragrance-free litter. As I mentioned earlier, cats are very sensitive to smells and everything gets absorbed more easily through their skin. I listed all these items mentioned here at:

TheRevolutionBlog.com/cleaning-resources.

KEEPING YOUR CHILDREN'S TOYS CLEAN

Every time I hear a story of someone cleaning a child's toy by soaking it in a solution of bleach and water or by wiping it down with a conventional disinfectant wipe, I cringe. There are plenty of safer and more natural options that will disinfect your children's toys just as well without the toxic harm to them. Kids usually put their toys in their mouths, which is one of the reasons they need to be disinfected on a regular basis.

You can use any of the following solutions safely to spray the toys down. You can either do a quick wipe or let the solutions sit for more disinfecting power. Soaking the toys in the solution for 5-20 minutes is also an option. Always rinse with clean water and dry the toys when you use any of these methods.

Equal parts vinegar and water.

3% Food grade Hydrogen Peroxide.

Equal parts vodka and water.

I do not recommend drug store hydrogen peroxide or rubbing alcohol in these applications because they have more additives in them that your kids could be sensitive to. You will still be rinsing all these solutions off after you soak them to avoid any irritation they could potentially cause. Certain kids' toys are also top rack dishwasher safe, by being placed in a dishwashing container or laundry bag, but make sure they are heat resistant first. If they are plush toys, put them in a laundry bag and throw them in the washing machine using the natural cleaning methods.

Don't use essential oils when cleaning your kid's toys.

KEEPING YOUR PRODUCE CLEAN

Produce can easily be cleaned using the **3% Food Grade Hydrogen Peroxide** cleaner and the lemon version of the **Citrus Vinegar Cleaner** as all ingredients in it are beneficial to washing produce. Plain water and vinegar is also an option if you do not want to use the citrus cleaner or do not have food grade hydrogen peroxide, which can be used alone to clean produce. Start by cleaning the sink basin by using one or both cleaners, then thoroughly spray the produce with one or both cleaners and let them sit in the sink for 10-20 minutes before rinsing under cold, preferably filtered water. Let the produce dry on clean dish towels. For items like potatoes or waxed fruit, you may want to also scrub with some baking soda. When drying leafy greens, pat them with a clean dish towel first, then run through a salad spinner. Once that's complete, put them back in their produce bag with a cloth napkin to help keep them crisp. Make sure your produce is completely dry before returning it to the fridge.

The reason this method is so effective is the same reason cited in the study under disinfecting surfaces. The two together kills virtually all Salmonella and E. coli along with other bacteria. Never pre-mix vinegar and hydrogen peroxide. Produce must always be sprayed one after another.

For a quick cleaning of a fruit or vegetable when you don't have time to soak and wait, just spray with either solution, wait about 30 seconds, then rinse, preferably with filtered water. Scrub with baking soda if needed. This quick method isn't as effective as letting the product soak a bit, but will still do a good job of getting the produce clean enough and safe to eat.

Cleaning your fruits and vegetables this way will also reduce pesticide residue in addition to killing harmful bacteria. Of course, the best way to reduce pesticide exposure is to buy organic whenever possible.

KEEPING YOUR CAR CLEAN

When it's time to take the green cleaning show on the road, the **Rosemary Lavender Cleaner** works great for wiping down the interior, dashboard, and windows of your car. To freshen upholstery, you can either use baking soda (which you vacuum up) or the **Fabric Refresher**. If you have leather seats, glycerin-based saddle soap is a recommended option for keeping them clean. Dashboards can be shined and protected with a little bit of coconut oil and orange essential oil buffed on using a microfiber cloth. To keep air fresh in the car, use a DIY baking soda sachet or charcoal air freshener.

It is said that the most environmentally friendly way to wash a car is to take it to a car wash because they use less water, have filter systems, and are required to use more environmentally friendly products. If you still want to clean your car at home, a basic car wash solution is $1/3$ cup distilled white vinegar mixed with one gallon of water. You can also add a few squirts of Castile soap if your car is especially dirty. Make sure you rinse, dry, and polish the car afterward with a lint-free polishing cloth.

KEEPING YOUR HOME PEST-FREE

Unfortunately, even a clean home can attract pests. Here are some of the safest and most environmentally friendly ways to get rid of them. Regularly using the **Pest Repellant House Spray** around doors and windows can help deter pests from entering your home in the first place.

Ants

Peppermint, tea tree, and citrus essential oils, and vinegar all deter ants. To use, spray or wipe a mixture of one or all oils on baseboards or other entry points. You can also place soaked cotton balls with that mixture in areas they may be attracted to. To kill ants, you can use a mixture of baking soda and powdered sugar in the areas where the ants hang out. The mixture attracts the ants then kills them. Once you notice there are no more ants headed toward the mixture, throw it out.

Spiders

The essential oils that repel spiders are lavender, citrus, peppermint, and tea tree, so using a spray or wiping mixture as you do with ants to help keep spiders, ants, roaches, mosquitoes, and many other pests away. Another spider repelling technique is to make a mixture of regular table salt and water then spray the same way.

Fruit flies

Make a simple fruit fly trap by putting a little apple cider vinegar (regular vinegar will not work) in a tall glass jar with a few drops of Castile soap. Secure plastic wrap to the top and poke a couple of holes through the film. They will be attracted to the smell of the apple cider vinegar. Once inside they will not be able to get out.

Fleas

Salting your floors and furniture with table salt then vacuuming up after several hours can dehydrate and kill flea eggs, but you must be persistent and do it regularly until the problem goes away. Keep your pets away until vacuumed up. To keep your dog or cat from attracting fleas, you can spray them with some apple cider vinegar or use it while giving them a bath. Essential oils can be effective at repelling fleas, but that does not mean they are safe to use on your pets, and extensive research should be done before trying this method.

You can also create a flea trap by filling a shallow dish with warm, soapy water and placing it directly under a night light overnight, then empty it the next morning. Repeat until your problem disappears.

Moths

There is no need to resort to toxic mothballs to keep moths away. Instead, use muslin bags filled with dried herbs such as cloves, cinnamon sticks, lavender, or cedar chips. These are all good moth repellents to keep in your closet. Make sure you vacuum your closet regularly. Ironing or freezing your clothes can help kill the eggs and larvae.

Keeping your home clean and vacuumed is the best general way to keep pests from entering and staying in your space. Keep your porch lights off when possible, as light attracts bugs. Make sure your home is well sealed by installing door sweeps, caulking windows, and repairing damaged screens. Store food in airtight containers and empty the garbage regularly. Put bay leaves and cotton balls with peppermint essential oil in your food pantry. The essential oils in this book all have pest repelling properties, so cleaning with them, spraying them around doorways and windows, and keeping soaked cotton balls in cabinets, etc. can help deter many pests. Cleaning with vinegar also repels many bugs.

If you have a pest problem that I do not address here, please do your research online for natural alternatives to try out before resorting to toxic chemical solutions. Food grade diatomaceous earth is also something you may want to consider, which is said to be a very effective and safe solution for getting rid of pests, particularly fleas in the carpet. Be careful if you have pets. Keep them away from all pest repelling methods.

KEEPING YOUR AIR AND WATER CLEAN

I am guessing since you are considering cleaning methods that reduce your toxic burden, that you are also interested in breathing clean air and drinking clean water.

CLEANING YOUR AIR

> The EPA found levels of VOCs to be 2 to 5 times higher inside homes than outside, regardless of where the home was located. The studies indicated that people using products that contained these compounds, like cleaning supplies, can be exposing themselves to very high pollutant levels, and elevated concentrations can persist in the air long after the activity is completed.

References mentioned in the preceding text box may be found at endnote 45.[45]

The good news is once you switch to green products they will drastically cut down your indoor air pollution. Besides opening windows, which is good to do regularly, the following methods will help keep the air in your home clean and reduce indoor air pollutants. For recommendations on the things listed visit **TheRevolutionBlog.com/cleaning-resources.**

Plants

Plants clean the air by breaking down airborne chemicals and neutralizing them. They can help clear known toxins like formaldehyde, benzene, xylene, carbon monoxide, and other volatile organic compounds (VOCs) that can be caused by toxic chemicals and off-gassing of furniture, fabrics, paint, carpeting, and other common materials.[46] Some of the best air cleaning plants that are also safe for pets are bamboo palm, spider plant, Boston fern, and areca.

Beeswax Candles and Himalayan Salt Lamps

Both beeswax candles and Himalayan salt lamps are said to clean the air by releasing negative ions. Pollen, dust, dirt, pollutants, and allergens in the air carry a positive charge. The negative ions neutralize positive ions so they are no longer airborne, making them good for people with asthma and allergies.[47] Negative ions contribute to reduced dust levels. As a bonus, negative ions are said to provide mood-boosting benefits as well.

HEPA Air Purifier

On the slightly more expensive side, you could get a HEPA air purifier to clean the air in your home. They work by forcing air through a fine mesh that traps harmful particles like pollen, dust mites, and dander. It is a bonus if your HEPA air filter also includes a charcoal layer to help reduce odors. If possible, use a vacuum with a HEPA filter instead of other filters or you will let a lot of the dust, dirt, and dander pass back into your home because it does not trap smaller particles like a HEPA filter. Remember to change the filter on your furnace regularly and clean your vents periodically.

CLEANING YOUR WATER

By not using unsafe chemical products, you are no longer contributing to contaminating groundwater with your cleaning supplies. Unfortunately, the water that comes into your home that you use for drinking, bathing, and cooking has the possibility of already being contaminated.

Now that you have spent time and effort getting the toxic chemicals out of your home, the last thing you want to do is drink them and bathe in them. Some of the worst things that can be contaminating your tap water are bacteria, VOCs, heavy metals, endocrine disrupting chemicals, chlorine, and fluoride.

Of course, the ideal solution would be a whole-house filter that can remove all contaminants. However, that is not a practical and cost-effective solution for everyone, and unfortunately, there are some contaminants that are hard to remove. At the very least, have a good quality filter on your kitchen sink and shower heads. I list some recommended options at TheRevolutionBlog.com/cleaning-resources. You want to make sure you filter out as much chlorine as you can while taking a shower, as chlorine can damage your hair, skin, and lungs while showering or bathing. Make sure you and your family are drinking and bathing in the purest water you possibly can.

Fluoride, which is voluntarily added to our municipal water systems, is of great concern, and it is very hard to find filters to remove it without also removing the good minerals needed for healthy water. The type of fluoride added to our water supply is not the naturally occurring kind. It is a toxic byproduct of the fertilizer and aluminum industry. The US Environmental Protection Agency (EPA) lists fluoride among about 100 chemicals for which there is "substantial evidence of developmental neurotoxicity."[48] Fluoride can damage fertility, destroy bones, cause early puberty in children, impair thyroid function, calcify the pineal gland, and much more. Something that was considered too toxic to dispose of any other way is being added to our drinking water under the veil that it helps prevent cavities. I am not here to argue whether fluoride helps fight cavities, but there are plenty of fluorinated toothpastes so the people who choose to use it can. But to be forced to regularly drink a toxic byproduct in our municipal water is something everyone in America should be up in arms about. Other countries have banned water fluoridation, including Norway, Sweden, Germany, Japan, Austria, Belgium, the Netherlands, Hungary, and China.[49] We should be doing whatever we can to speak up and act against this. It is about letting people have a choice on whether they want to expose themselves to fluoride because right now we don't have a choice!

Fluoride in our water is something you should consider more. It is serious! I also provide more info on it and what you can do about it at TheRevolutionBlog.com/get-involved.

CHAPTER 6. TIPS AND MISCELLANEOUS CLEANING HACKS

Okay, because I think it is so important to tell you every little thing I learned on this green cleaning path, this chapter contains a bunch of miscellaneous tips and cleaning hacks I feel are worth sharing.

Using and storing your microfiber cloths: I recommend buying enough microfiber cloths so you only have to wash them every 2-4 weeks. The kind I purchased has three colors; yellow, green, and blue. I use yellow for bathrooms, blue for general dusting/cleaning, and green in the kitchen. I also found cute, small, color-matching storage boxes and laundry baskets at the dollar store for them. I used to wash them separately but now I wash them in the same load using 3 different laundry bags that contain the microfibers and keep the debris from spreading.

Keep the ingredients and tools to make the recipes together in a container. I suggest keeping the tools like measuring cup and funnel as well as the ingredients you use most, in the same storage bin or container. This way it's easy to grab and will save you time in gathering all the supplies.

Don't wear shoes in the house. Shoes carry in bacteria, toxins, and dirt from the outside, which is exactly what you are trying to get out of your home. I store regularly worn shoes in my coat closet instead of my regular closet to make sure I take them off and put them on at the door. You could also use something like a shoe cubby to store your shoes near the door you use the most.

Preserve your distilled water. Using grapefruit seed extract can be very helpful if you are opening a bottle of distilled water that you will not be finishing right away. Just add 3-5 drops, depending on how much is left and it will help preserve it by helping to keep the bacteria away.

Keep your bathroom smelling good. To keep your bathroom smelling fresh put a few drops of essential oil on the inside of your toilet paper roll every time you change it.

Infuse your vinegar. Instead of using essential oils to create a scented vinegar, you can infuse white distilled vinegar with orange and lemon peels. Place the peels in a jar with vinegar, shake, and let infuse for two or more weeks. Strain out the peels, and use equal parts of the infused vinegar in place of regular vinegar in the cleaning recipes.

Clean your toothbrush! People's mouths are full of bacteria, but most people rarely clean their toothbrushes. I recommend you throw your toothbrush in the dishwasher at least once a week and spritz or soak the brush head with the **3% Hydrogen Peroxide Cleaner** between uses.

Clean your hair brushes and combs. Hair brushes and combs are other items that seem to get neglected when it comes to cleaning. Start by removing any unwanted hair, using a comb and scissors if needed. You can soak plastic combs and brushes in a mixture of equal parts hot water and white vinegar for a couple of minutes, then rinse and lay out to dry. For wooden combs and brushes, which are what I use, wipe them down with a cloth dampened with apple cider vinegar, then moisturize them with a little bit of olive, coconut, or almond oil.

Clean your makeup brushes. The **Moisturizing Hand Soap** is great for cleaning makeup brushes, as it is both cleansing and softening. Just wash them with the hand soap and hot water. Remove excess water then lay flat to dry on a cloth or paper towel. Plain Castile soap and water can be used as well.

Clean your small electronics regularly. Make sure to clean your phone, tablets, remotes, and other small electronics regularly as they harbor many germs. Clean them at least once a week with the **Electronic Cleaner** and microfiber cloth.

Wipe down your makeup. The exterior of makeup is also a great thing to clean with the **Electronic Cleaner** or plain alcohol and a cotton pad.

Use 3% food grade hydrogen peroxide and vodka in the medicine cabinet. I personally choose to keep small bottles of 3% food grade hydrogen peroxide and vodka inside my medicine cabinet instead of keeping bottles of drugstore hydrogen peroxide and rubbing alcohol. They can be used in the same ways and are better for you because they don't have the additives.

Natural enzymes for stains. The one thing DIY natural cleaning products do not provide are natural enzymes that can be found in some store bought natural cleaners. It is not a bad idea to have some natural liquid enzyme laundry detergent or stain remover around if needed for stains on clothes, carpet, or upholstery.

Shake ingredients to blend well. Before each use, it is a good idea to shake the liquid products you make to evenly distribute the ingredients since they don't have the fillers conventional products do to keep the ingredients evenly distributed. They will still do a good job even if you forget.

Clean your utensils when away from soap and water. If you need to clean items like silverware, knives, cutting boards, etc. when away from soap and water, **3% Food Grade Hydrogen Peroxide Cleaner** and a rag will work. Just do not use on silver or copper.

Clean your washing machine. To deep clean your washing machine, run a cycle with two cups of baking soda on the hot, heavy cycle. Repeat the same cycle using two cups of vinegar instead of baking soda. Wipe down the inside of the drum when done.

Clean your dishwasher. Sometimes you need to clean your dishwasher. To do so, put fill a glass with vinegar place on the top shelf and run through a long hot empty cycle. To further deodorize and get rid of stains sprinkle baking soda on the bottom and run a short hot empty cycle. This method only needs to be done once or twice a year.

Clean your electric kettle or coffee pot. To clean an electric kettle or coffee pot, run through a cycle with distilled vinegar and equal parts water.

Remove hard water buildup on the shower head. If you have hard water build up on your shower head, put vinegar in a plastic bag and secure to your showerhead with a rubber band or if it is easier for you unscrew your showerhead, take it off and put it in a cup of vinegar. Let it sit overnight. By morning, the build-up should be gone. This method works great on chrome and stainless steel, but be careful of use on other finishes, as it may cause part of the finish to dissolve.

Get rid of rust. Put a vinegar-soaked paper towel over the area for 15 plus minutes. I find baking soda and **3% Hydrogen Peroxide Cleaner** combined also works very well, depending on the surface.

Clean your whiteboard. The **Electronic Cleaner**, which is equal parts alcohol and water, works great as a whiteboard cleaner and can even be used to get pen ink and permanent marker off surfaces.

Replace the erasers. You can replace those little white sponges by wetting a corner of a microfiber cloth and dipping it in baking soda. Great for removing scuff marks and spots from walls. Make sure to spot test before using.

Reuse your candles. You can easily reuse the jars you make your candles in by freezing them so the wax pops out. You can also cut out the wick and re-melt the wax next time you make more candles.

Store cleaning supplies in each room where they will be used. It is a good idea to have multiple sets of cleaning supplies that you can distribute in the areas where they will be used, like one in the kitchen and in the bathroom. That way you do not need to haul everything around and everything is close if you need to do a quick clean up. Store your microfiber cloths in the room you will be using them.

Recycle! Next to every trash can, have a second container for recyclable items, making it very easy to remember to recycle.

Easy shaker for baking soda. Storing your baking soda in glass parmesan cheese shakers makes it very easy and convenient to use. You can also reuse old plastic ones.

Keep your cleaning tools clean. Throw dish brushes in the dishwasher weekly to clean. For plastic broom heads, dust pans, and other brushes, start by using a pen or chopstick to remove unwanted debris between the bristles. Fill a bucket with hot water and $1/4$ cup of sodium percarbonate or ½ cup **3% Hydrogen Peroxide Cleaner** let soak for 20 minutes before rinsing and laying out to dry. You can also wipe down the outside of your cleaning products and tools using a microfiber cloth dipped in any of the cleaning solutions.

Keeping mops clean. Only use mops that have a mop head cover that can be thrown in the wash. Sponge mops, especially, are breeding grounds for everything you don't want to clean with and using a bucket spreads germs. Use a flat head mop and spray cleaner or steam mop instead. Keep multiple mop head covers on hand and throw your mop head covers in the wash with soap nuts and sodium percarbonate or **3% Hydrogen Peroxide Cleaner** and baking soda on the hot cycle.

Clean your vacuum. Clean by emptying the canister regularly and washing any filters as instructed. To clean the powerhead, you can use a pair of scissors to cut off and remove any strings or hair. You can clean the attachments by soaking them in warm, soapy water and letting dry or by wiping down with a cleaner and a cloth.

Protect your glass cleaning bottles. A drink koozie is great way to protect your glass cleaning bottles, if you are worried about them breaking.

Label your products with recipes. Labeling the bottle with the full recipe to have it readily available when it is time to remake the product. You can also mark fill lines with a marker, tape or label placement so you don't need to measure every time.

Organize your cleaning lists. Make cleaning checklists for what you clean daily, weekly, monthly, and yearly to help you stay on track.

Enjoy your cleaning time! Listening to audiobooks can be a great way to pass the time while cleaning. You can learn something new and complete your tasks at the same time.

CHAPTER 7. PROPERLY DISPOSING OF ITEMS

After learning about the toxicity in many commercial cleaning products, you probably want to get rid of most, if not all of them as you switch to the green cleaning products. However, because they are toxic, you need to be sure to dispose of them properly to avoid causing further harm to the environment, yourself, or others.

Statement was taken directly from the EPA website below:

*"Leftover household products that contain corrosive, toxic, ignitable, or reactive ingredients are considered to be household hazardous waste (HHW). Products, such as paints, **cleaners**, oils, batteries, and pesticides that contain potentially hazardous ingredients require special care when you dispose of them.*

Improper disposal of HHW can include pouring them down the drain, on the ground, into storm sewers, or in some cases putting them out with the trash. The dangers of such disposal methods might not be immediately obvious, but improper disposal of these wastes can pollute the environment and pose a threat to human health. Many communities in the United States offer a variety of options for conveniently and safely managing HHW".

In some cases, getting rid of chemicals and other hazardous materials can be a costly and time-consuming process, which is unfortunate because it keeps most people from doing it properly. Every city is different, so you need to research your city guidelines specifically, as some cities make it easier than others. You may even decide your old cleaners need to sit on a garage or closet shelf until you have the time to deal with them, which I think is a much better idea than using them up. The point is you need to dispose of them safely. Being overwhelmed with what to do with all your old cleaners should not stop you from moving forward with green cleaning. Box them up and make room for your green cleaners, then safely store them and other hazardous products until you are ready to dispose of them properly.

Call your city to see if they offer any pickup services or if there is a specific hazardous waste disposal plant you can take them to. You can also use your search engine to search for hazardous waste disposal in your city.

Other hazardous items you need to be careful of when disposing of:

Compact fluorescent light bulbs (CFLs) contain mercury, which can be very dangerous to human health along with the environment, and need to be properly disposed of as well. These light bulbs are very toxic when broken, so when collecting them for recycling, it is recommended to store and package them to minimize lamp breakage. Most major home improvement stores will take them.

Expired medicine is another item that is important to properly dispose of. Most hospitals and drug stores will take expired or unwanted medicine back to properly dispose of them as part of a medicine take-back program. Never flush or pour medicines down the drain as they can end up contaminating our food and water supplies and are not easily removed by waste-water treatment plants or septic systems. It is also never a good idea for medications to just be thrown in the trash as they are still chemically active and can be released into the environment.

In many states, improperly disposing of what is hazardous waste, including the items listed above, is a direct violation of hazardous waste laws and can result in large fines and criminal prosecution.

Recycle, recycle, recycle! There are so many items that do not need to end up in the landfill. Do your research to find the best and easiest ways to recycle in your neighborhood, and do your part. I have more information on where to recycle and properly dispose of hazardous materials at TheRevolutionBlog.com/cleaning-references.

CHAPTER 8. CONSCIOUS CONSUMERISM

While I may have written a book on DIY cleaning product recipes I still believe in supporting the companies that are innovative and look for cutting-edge solutions when it comes to benefiting us and our planet.

The biggest and most influential vote you have is in how you spend your dollar. What products, services, and companies do you choose to support?

Not very many of us are made aware or pay attention to the impact the products we regularly purchase have on our future. The world and the consumer marketplace will benefit if we start paying attention, educating ourselves, and spending our money in ways that better align with our personal values.

I am not here to tell you what your values are, I am just suggesting that if more people spend their money to reflect their values, it will make a positive and powerful impact. Do more research on the products you regularly purchase and the companies you purchase from.

Do you want to support local businesses, cruelty-free brands, companies that have environmentally friendly practices, non-toxic chemical-free products, organic farming, local farming, fair trade, fair wages, or all the above? The list goes on and on. Pick what is most important to you and start taking steps in that direction.

This does not mean 100% of what you buy must be consciously purchased. Take more of an 80/20 approach and start with some of your regularly purchased items by learning more about the ingredients and the companies that manufacture them. Start looking for more sustainable and ethically sourced goods. When you pay just a little bit of attention, it is amazing to realize how much your buying power can accomplish to make things better.

By standing up and voting with our dollar, we force companies to change or innovate. Companies will not spend the money on research and new product development if there is not any consumer demand for it.

You may say, "I don't have the money to spend consciously since the products are usually more expensive," but if you spend according to your values, you will not only value your things more but spend much less on what you don't truly need, which will ultimately save you money.

What will happen if people start spending their money to reflect their values? Big companies that have not supported the consumers' best interest will either need to evolve to the needs and wants of the conscious consumer or flounder because business is about meeting consumer needs. New jobs will be created under companies that align with this new consumer mindset. New industries and products will be born to support this new paradigm. These companies will continue to grow and become bigger and continue to be supported if they maintain the values and needs of their customers. The key is not to take your money out of the economic system. It is about your money changing things by changing where it goes.

We as individuals have the power to help redistribute the wealth and influence change by choosing who gets our money!

CHAPTER 9. CONCLUSION – HOW GREEN CLEANING IMPACTED MY LIFE

Thank you very much for taking the time to read this book! As you can probably tell, I am passionate about green cleaning because of the profound positive impact it has had on my life, and I hope it will have the same profound positive impact on yours. Although I cannot credit green cleaning for all the changes I experienced, it was a huge starting point for me.

When I first moved out on my own, I did not do a good job of cleaning or maintaining my first apartment. It seemed like it was always a disaster because I was not motivated to clean and didn't really know how. When I did clean, I got what I refer to as a "cleaning hangover;" where I got headaches, felt light-headed, and extra lethargic. This problem with me not cleaning seemed to be compounded with the fact that I just didn't feel in control of my own life. I felt victimized by life. I took very little responsibility for where I was in my life and always tended to blame everything on the things going on around me.

Reading the book "The 7 Habits of Highly Effective People" by Stephen R. Covey, was one of the first steps I took that motivated change in my life (also, I highly recommend to anyone who has not read it yet). A quote directly from his book that really hit home and influenced me was:

"As human beings, we are responsible for our own lives. Our behavior is a function of our decisions, not our conditions. We can subordinate feelings to values. We have the initiative and the responsibility to make things happen". - Stephen R. Covey

In his book, The 7 Habits of Highly Effective People, Stephen R. Covey talks about proactive vs reactive people. Stating proactive people's behavior is a product of their own conscious choice based on their values instead of conditions vs. reactive people whose behavior is based on their conditions instead of their values. He also talks about circle of concern vs. circle of influence. Stating reactive people focus on the circle of concern and things they can't change vs. proactive people who focus on their circle of influence and things they can change.

Before reading that book, I was a reactive person. I always felt things were being done *to me* instead of *because of me*. The book helped shift my perspective, and I was motivated to start taking a more proactive approach with my behavior.

Many years later, when I started to learn about green cleaning, it really hit home for me that this was a great way I could focus on my circle of influence and be proactive by putting my values first to make a change in my life. What I didn't know was how big of an impact it would have on my life. I found making my own cleaners was not only easy, but it was also fun. I started to clean more because I enjoyed it more. I no longer experienced the cleaning hangover symptoms that had made me feel light-headed, lethargic, and gave me headaches. Instead, I felt refreshed and invigorated every time I used my homemade cleaning products.

Now don't get me wrong, even though I do so much better than I used to, there are still times I let my place get dirty. That's how I know the things mentioned in this book work. Even after I let my house get extra dirty and grimy, I can still get it sparking clean and fresh again using just the products, tools, and methods listed in this book; without any help from conventional cleaners. After green cleaning, my home feels more like a sanctuary, a place I can rest and recover without being assaulted by a bunch of unnecessary toxins.

Green cleaning was just a starting point for me, though. From there, I looked more into my personal care items, from skincare to personal hygiene and makeup. I studied the ingredients, started to make more items myself, and became more cautious about what I purchased. I think most people in my life would agree that, after that shift, my hair, skin, and makeup (yes, I still wear it) have never looked better (a book on my lessons learned with green beauty will be coming soon).

Then, I started to make changes to my diet. I didn't go on any crazy diets or restrictive programs like I had in the past. I just started to care more about the nutritional impact of the foods and ingredients I used, and how they were sourced. I ate more natural foods and made sure the foods I purchased were not full of hard to pronounce ingredients, pesticides, or chemical preservatives. Not only was it easy because I did not restrict myself, but the food tasted so much better, and more importantly, I felt so much better eating them.

These changes did not happen overnight. These changes took years to fully integrate and implement, but the results have been so worth it.

The more I got these toxins out of my everyday life, the more motivated I became. Through the process, my mood improved and I started to be kinder and more understanding towards people. I am now the healthiest I have ever been and rarely get sick anymore. My skin finally cleared after struggling with acne my entire teenage and young adult life, and people often compliment me on my healthy glow.

I am not perfect and choose to take an 80/20 or 90/10 approach to most things in life. I just have the knowledge and understanding now to make better choices and decisions for myself when I choose to. I do not live like some off the grid hippy (no offense to off the grid hippies, they are awesome!). I do, however, make a conscious effort to do things on a regular basis that have a positive impact on myself and the environment.

I know many of you are reading this book because you have some awareness that green cleaning can be helpful. You are probably already doing several positive things in your life for yourself and for the world around you. I hope this book gave you some simple tools to make your life even better with healthier cleaning products. My life changes may have been more dramatic as I had a long way to go. You may already be well on your way.

As mentioned in the beginning of my book, the information, recipes, and possible impact, are all things I wish I had learned about and implemented earlier in my life, so these profound changes could have happened even sooner. I am looking to expand my circle of influence by passing on to you what I have learned over the years. Whether it is brand new information to you or it just increases your understanding about the importance of green cleaning, please understand how valuable this information can be to the world if it gets in enough hands and enough people are willing to start making small changes that can lead to big steps for humanity. This message will only go as far as the readers of this book take it.

Now it's your turn. Crawl, walk, or run but take that first or next step towards a healthier life and a better world!

10 Ways to Get Involved and Inspire Change

By starting to green clean you are already taking a big step toward doing your part for a better planet. If you are interested in taking your impact even further and spreading the message, even more, the ideas below are a great way to do that. You, of course, do not need to do all these things at once (unless you are really passionate and have the time). Pick just one or a few of them you feel the most inspired by and start there.

If you are inspired to do something that I mentioned but still don't know quite how to do it or where to start, visit **TheRevolutionBlog.com/get-involved**, where I provide more information, links, and resources on how to accomplish all these things.

Some people are going to say that I am only encouraging people to spread the message of the book so it sells well. Of course I desire the book to do well! More than that, though, I desire for people to quit using these toxic chemical products that can be carcinogenic and cause breathing and other health problems. I desire for people to stop contributing to the pollution of our soil and waterways through their cleaning products that are causing serious harm and contamination to aquatic life. I desire for us to stop being such a wasteful society by not allowing so many items end up in the landfill that don't need to. I desire for a better and healthier world for all!

Tupac Shakur once said, *"I'm not saying I'm gonna change the world, but I guarantee that I will spark the brain that will change the world."*

That is my wish with this book; to spark the brains of the people that are going to run with it and use the information to do their part in creating a better and healthier world for all!

#1 Spread the Message!

The first and most important thing you can do, besides taking action on these items in the book, is to spread the message!

Encourage others to read this book and look more into the impact that conventional cleaners have on people and the environment. Post recipes, cleaning tips, and other things you learned in the book and found to be valuable in your social media posts. Take pictures of the products you make and post them online using #EASYGREENCLEANING. If you make online videos, consider doing videos showing how you make some of the green cleaners and/or how you use them.

Per the copyright notice in the front of the book, you have permission to use up to 5% of this book content for your own use if you credit the book and place a link to the book in the post.

#2 SHOP CONSCIOUSLY!

Make a list of all the products in your home you purchase on a regular basis. Place a star next to the items you are most interested in switching to a greener product first. Do some research on what you would like to purchase or make to replace the product with. Look at the ingredients and the company that makes the product. Make sure these products and companies align with your values and what you want to start bringing into your life. Repeat until you replace all the products you starred on the list and see if there are any more you would like to add.

Do some additional research on what it takes to shop ethically and responsibly so it can carry over to more areas of your life as well.

#3 REDUCE, REUSE, RECYCLE

REDUCE: Start being more conscious about the things you bring into your home and donate things you no longer use. Cut down on the things that come into your home that are wasteful, like junk mail.

REUSE: Start replacing disposable items with things like reusable stainless steel or glass water bottles. Start taking your own reusable coffee cup to your coffee shop to have them refill it. If you get food on the go a lot, carry your own reusable cutlery, start using cloth napkins instead of paper at home, and take your reusable shopping bags when you go into the store.

RECYCLE: A lot more things can be recycled than you think; you just need to know how and where. Look into what and where you can recycle in your local city. Create containers in your house to store different recyclable items until you can take them to the recycling facility or have them picked up by your garbage service. Do your best to purchase more items in bulk with recyclable containers in efforts to cut down on waste. If you have the ability, start composting in your yard or research if there is a way to start a community compost in your area.

#4 GET YOUR COMMUNITY INVOLVED

Now that you know how and where you can recycle, why not make flyers you can pass around to your neighbors and community to share the information. You can also post it at your local grocery stores and other community groups or places you attend if they have bulletin boards for flyers. You can even include your favorite recipes and tips from the book on the flyer as well.

Contact your local schools, day care centers, churches, and other organizations to inquire about the cleaning products they use. See if you can get whoever is in charge, a copy of the book. See if they are willing to be gathering places for smaller, harder to recycle items so people have a more central place they can go before it is distributed out to different recycling facilities. You can also see if they are interested in holding workshops or seminars for people that are interested in learning more about green living.

#5 MAKE PRODUCTS FOR FRIENDS AND FAMILY

Consider gifting people copies of the book. To give them the extra incentive, consider making them a couple of your favorite recipes to give along with some reusable cleaning cloths so they have no excuse to not try it.

When people you know first move out on their own or move into a new home, consider making them welcome baskets that contain a copy of the book along with tools and ingredients that would help them start green cleaning right away. These baskets also make great holiday gifts.

Have a Green Cleaning Party at your house with your friends where they can learn and make the recipes in the book while having some food, drinks, and a good time. You could have everyone pitch in potluck style by each bringing a food item and an ingredient.

#6 GET INVOLVED WITH ORGANIZATIONS THAT SUPPORT THE CAUSE

Donate or volunteer with consumer rights groups and other organizations that support the cause of informing us and helping us lobby for environmental and safety changes in the government. I will include the ones I recommend at the TheRevolutionBlog.com/get-involved so you can do more research and see which ones you would like to get involved with and support.

#7 KNOW WHAT IS GOING ON

I am very careful of how and where I get my information. It is much easier to avoid many topics rather than face them head-on, but when it comes to things that could impact you and your family, it is important to know what is going on.

Keep yourself well-informed of the current laws on chemical regulation and reform. Know what is going on regarding lobby groups and new laws passing on what people want to regulate or deregulate in the chemical and food industry. Learn more about what is in all the products you buy, not just your cleaning supplies, and how they can impact you and your family.

#8 SPEAK OUT

Contact city officials, sign petitions, write your congress representatives, contact the companies, go to town hall meetings, and tell manufacturers you demand to know what is in the products you purchase. If there is a chemical or chemicals you are particularly passionate about them removing, give them pressure to remove those chemicals and overhaul the approval process of letting these chemicals into our products in the first place.

While you are doing all of that, tell them to get the fluoride out of our water!

#9 START OR JOIN A GROUP

Start or join a meetup or other group in your area of like-minded people with the intention of improving the world! Or, at least, play your role in a group of people who are inspired to make a difference. When a group of like-minded people come together with the intention to impact change, profound things can happen!

Make it your group mission to bring different issues to light and brainstorm on ways to make a difference!

#10 JOIN THE REVOLUTION!

Visit TheRevolutionBlog.com to join a like-minded online community and be kept up to date on more ways to live a healthier greener life, new book releases, additional resources, and get information on other causes and issues that impact us and what we can do about them! While you're there get our **FREE 5 Step Guide to a Healthier Greener Life!**

If not you, then who? If not now, then when?

"Be the change you wish to see in the world." – Gandhi

What did you think of the book Easy Green Cleaning?

Thank you so much for taking the time to read this book and for starting your process on the journey to a better, safer, planet. **If you found this information helpful and valuable** in your life, **please take just a few moments to leave a review**. It would mean so much to me!

Your feedback and support will not only help spread the message of the book **it will benefit people who are considering purchasing it** so they know if it will be the right book for them. Leaving reviews will also help **support the creation of future books and projects on greener living** and healthier lifestyle choices.

I want you, as the reader to know just **how important your review is**, and to thank you in advance for taking the initiative to leave one. **To leave a review** just go to the page where you purchased the book, click write a review in the reviews section then click submit. **It is that easy!** Again, **thank you** for doing your part in spreading this important message and **I wish you all the best with your future success** in living a healthier and greener life!

List of Helpful Links for Easy Reference:

Visit the blog to get involved, stay up to date on new content and receive our **FREE 5 Step Guide to a Healthier Greener Life!** TheRevolutionBlog.com

Visit the resources link for a list of all ingredients, tools, and products listed in the book and where to buy. TheRevolutionBlog.com/cleaning-resources

Visit the references link for book and documentary recommendations as well as more in-depth information on the ideas stated in this book and other helpful links to help you on your journey. TheRevolutionBlog.com/cleaning-references

Visit the link below for more information on how to get involved and inspire change.

TheRevolutionBlog.com/get-involved

Learn more about the causes this book chooses to support.

TheRevolutionBlog.com/give-back

Learn more about Revolution Book Series and upcoming books.

RevolutionBookSeries.com

A special thank you to all the readers who took the time to read this book and by doing that are helping to implement steps for change!

Visit **TheRevolutionBlog.com** for more healthy, eco-friendly living tips and receive our FREE **5 Step Guide to a Healthier Greener Life**!

Revolution Book Series' mission is to publish books that inspire and effect conscious change.

About the Author:

Elizabeth Hemmings always dreamed of publishing books that could positively impact people's lives. This book is her first step in doing that.

She is passionate about health, the environment, and creating a world where people learn to be kinder and more understanding of each other.

She is not perfect but she does her best to play her role in all of that.

END NOTES

[1] "How to Reduce Your Paper Towel Use - The Paperless Project - Join the grassroots movement." The Paperless Project. Accessed September 18, 2017. http://www.thepaperlessproject.com/how-to-reduce-your-paper-towel-use/.

[2] "Banish the Paper Towel." Banish the Paper Towel | The Energy Co-op. Accessed September 25, 2017. https://www.theenergy.coop/community/blog/banish-paper-towel.

[3] Madrigal, Alexis. "Humans Have Made, Found or Used Over 50 Million Unique Chemicals." Wired. September 09, 2009. Accessed June 07, 2017. https://www.wired.com/2009/09/humans-have-made-found-or-used-over-50-million-unique-chemicals/.

[4] Ibid.

[5] DeAndrea, Richard. *A Holistic Living Guide*. 1st ed. 2010. Accessed July 31, 2017. https://books.google.com/books?id=WN92Ba51bhcC&printsec=frontcover&source=gbs_ge_summary_r&cad=0#v=onepage&q&f=false.

[6] "Poisoning Prevention." Centers for Disease Control and Prevention. April 28, 2016. Accessed June 19, 2017. https://www.cdc.gov/safechild/poisoning/index.html.

[7] "Department of Health." The Facts About Chlorine. Accessed June 08, 2017. https://www.health.ny.gov/environmental/emergency/chemical_terrorism/chlorine_general.htm.

[8] Hattersley, Joseph G. "The negative health effects of chlorine." Journal of Orthomolecular medicine 15.2 (2000): 89-95.

[9] Ibid.

[10] "Tox Town - Volatile Organic Compounds (VOCs) - Toxic chemicals and environmental health risks where you live and work - Text Version." U.S. National Library of Medicine. Accessed June 12, 2017. https://toxtown.nlm.nih.gov/text_version/chemicals.php?id=31.

[11] Ibid.

[12] "Tox Town - Phthalates - Toxic chemicals and environmental health risks where you live and work - Text Version." U.S. National Library of Medicine. Accessed June 09, 2017. https://toxtown.nlm.nih.gov/text_version/chemicals.php?id=24.

[13] Meeker, John D., Sheela Sathyanarayana, and Shanna H. Swan. "Phthalates and other additives in plastics: human exposure and associated health outcomes."

Philosophical Transactions of the Royal Society of London B: Biological Sciences. July 27, 2009. Accessed June 12, 2017. http://rstb.royalsocietypublishing.org/content/364/1526/2097.short.

[14] Ibid.

[15] Singer, Natasha. "Labels Can Hide the Presence of Phthalates." The New York Times. July 07, 2005. Accessed June 09, 2017. http://www.nytimes.com/2005/07/07/fashion/thursdaystyles/labels-can-hide-the-presence-of-phthalates.html?_r=0.

[16] Ibid

[17] "Department of Health." The Facts About Ammonia. Accessed June 12, 2017. https://www.health.ny.gov/environmental/emergency/chemical_terrorism/ammonia_tech.htm.

[18] Ibid.

[19] "Severe Lung Injury after Exposure to Chloramine Gas from Household Cleaners — NEJM." New England Journal of Medicine. Accessed June 12, 2017. http://www.nejm.org/doi/full/10.1056/NEJM199909093411115#t=article.

[20] "What causes autism? Exploring the environmental contribution : Current Opinion in Pediatrics." LWW. Accessed June 12, 2017. http://journals.lww.com/co-pediatrics/Abstract/2010/04000/What_causes_autism__Exploring_the_environmental.17.aspx.

[21] Meeker, John D., Sheela Sathyanarayana, and Shanna H. Swan. "Phthalates and other additives in plastics: human exposure and associated health outcomes." Philosophical Transactions of the Royal Society of London B: Biological Sciences. July 27, 2009. Accessed June 12, 2017. http://rstb.royalsocietypublishing.org/content/364/1526/2097.short.

[22] Fragranced consumer products: Chemicals emitted, ingredients unlisted. Accessed June 12, 2017. http://www.sciencedirect.com/science/article/pii/S0195925510001125.

[23] Fragranced consumer products and undisclosed ingredients. Accessed June 12, 2017. http://www.sciencedirect.com/science/article/pii/S0195925508000899.

[24] Dodson, Robin E., Marcia Nishioka, Laurel J. Standley, Laura J. Perovich, Julia G. Brody, and Ruthann A. Udel. "Endocrine Disruptors and Asthma-Associated Chemicals in Consumer Products." Environmental Health Perspectives 120, no. 7 (July 2012): 935. Accessed June 12, 2017.

http://search.proquest.com/openview/03729ed8cf5a37bedf24215c3293c41f/1?pq-origsite=gscholar&cbl=48869.

[25] "Why Are These Male Fish Growing Eggs?" National Geographic. July 07, 2017. Accessed July 07, 2017. http://news.nationalgeographic.com/2016/02/160203-feminized-fish-endocrine-disruption-hormones-wildlife-refuges/.

[26] Ibid.

[27] "Ozone Pollution." EPA. Accessed February 18, 2018

[28] "Chemistry in the Sunlight : Feature Articles." NASA. Accessed July 07, 201y7. https://earthobservatory.nasa.gov/Features/ChemistrySunlight/chemistry_sunlight3.php.

[29] "Good Up High Bad Nearby - What is Ozone?" Good Up High Bad Nearby - What is Ozone? Accessed July 07, 2017. https://airnow.gov/index.cfm?action=gooduphigh.index.

[30] What is Harmful Algal Bloom. (n.d.). Retrieved July 07, 2017, from http://www.noaa.gov/what-is-harmful-algal-bloom

[31] Learn about Dioxin. (2017, March 22). Retrieved July 07, 2017, from https://www.epa.gov/dioxin/learn-about-dioxin

[32] Henschler, Dietrich. "Toxicity of Chlorinated Organic Compounds: Effects of the Introduction of Chlorine in Organic Molecules." Angewandte Chemie International Edition. December 22, 2003. Accessed July 25, 2017. http://onlinelibrary.wiley.com/doi/10.1002/anie.199419201/abstract.

[33] "Formaldehyde and Cancer Risk." National Cancer Institute. Accessed September 07, 2017. https://www.cancer.gov/about-cancer/causes-prevention/risk/substances/formaldehyde/formaldehyde-fact-sheet.

[34] Park, J., L. M. Kamendulis, and J. E. Klaunig. "Effects of 2-butoxyethanol on hepatic oxidative damage." Toxicology letters. January 05, 2002. Accessed September 07, 2017. https://www.ncbi.nlm.nih.gov/pubmed/11738267.

[35] "Toxic Substances Portal - Sodium Hydroxide." Centers for Disease Control and Prevention. October 21, 2014. Accessed September 07, 2017. https://www.atsdr.cdc.gov/MMG/MMG.asp?id=246&tid=45.

[36] Commissioner, Office Of the. "Consumer Updates - 5 Things to Know About Triclosan." U S Food and Drug Administration Home Page. Accessed September 07, 2017. https://www.fda.gov/ForConsumers/ConsumerUpdates/ucm205999.htm.

[37] "Body Burden: The Pollution in Newborns." EWG. Accessed September 07, 2017. http://www.ewg.org/research/body-burden-pollution-newborns#.WbGs8NOGOHp.

[38] Hulett, Jessica. "6 Disposable Cleaning Alternatives That Save $250." Dealnews. September 03, 2015. Accessed September 19, 2017. https://www.dealnews.com/features/Are-You-Throwing-Away-Cash-with-Disposable-Cleaning-Products/550377.html.

[39] Jennifer, Jason Says, Brad Says, Jennifer Says, Nellie Says, Janell Says, Megan Says, Jennifer Chait Says, Cricket Says, Mandy Says, Jenuinearticle Says, and Martane Says. "Home." Growing a Green Family. May 22, 2017. Accessed September 19, 2017. http://www.growingagreenfamily.com/ditch-paper-towels-and-save-1000-in-five-years/.

[40] Sumner, Susan, Dr. *Science News*, August 29, 1996. Accessed July 28, 2017.

[41] "Toothbrush Fecal Matter." Discovery. September 18, 2014. Accessed September 07, 2017. http://www.discovery.com/tv-shows/mythbusters/mythbusters-database/fecal-matter-on-toothbrush/.

[42] Pritchard, Charlotte. "Is the toilet seat really the dirtiest place in the home?" BBC News. November 17, 2012. Accessed September 25, 2017. http://www.bbc.com/news/magazine-20324304.

[43] Cardinale, Massimiliano, Dominik Kaiser, Tillmann Lueders, Sylvia Schnell, and Markus Egert. "Microbiome analysis and confocal microscopy of used kitchen sponges reveal massive colonization by Acinetobacter , Moraxella and Chryseobacterium species." Nature News. July 19, 2017. Accessed September 25, 2017. https://www.nature.com/articles/s41598-017-06055-9.

[44] "5 Surprising Things You Don't Know About Air Fresheners - Air Freshener Health Risks | AGA." Grandparents.com. Accessed September 07, 2017. http://www.grandparents.com/health-and-wellbeing/health/are-air-fresheners-bad-for-you.

[45] "Volatile Organic Compounds' Impact on Indoor Air Quality." EPA. April 19, 2017. Accessed September 07, 2017. https://www.epa.gov/indoor-air-quality-iaq/volatile-organic-compounds-impact-indoor-air-quality.

[46] TailSmart, Adam Trainor Says, Ashley Says, Hypersensitive Says, Betty H. Says, Julia Says, Cindy Says, Steph Says, Candelario Says, and Rachy Says. "11 Detoxifying Plants that are Safe for Cats and Dogs." TailSmart. February 22, 2016. Accessed September 07, 2017. http://www.tailsmart.com/11-detoxifying-plants-that-are-safe-for-cats-and-dogs/.

[47] Mann, Denise. "Negative Ions Create Positive Vibes." WebMD. Accessed September 19, 2017. http://www.webmd.com/balance/features/negative-ions-create-positive-vibes#1.

[48] W. Mundy1, S. Padilla1, T. Shafer1, M. Gilbert1, J. Breier1,2, J. Cowden1, K. Crofton1, D. Herr1, K. Jensen1, K. Raffaele3, N. Radio4, and K. Schumacher5. *Building a Database of Developmental Neurotoxicants: Evidence from Human and Animal Studies*. PDF. Pittsburgh, PA: US EPA.

[49] " Fluoridation status of some countries." Fluoridation status of some countries. Accessed July 31, 2017. http://www.fluoridation.com/c-country.htm.

Made in the USA
Monee, IL
10 December 2019